THE GREATEST OF ALL SCIENCES:
TO KNOW ONE'S SELF

*Grant unto us, O Lord, the knowledge of
ourselves without which we can neither rightly
repent nor seek to amend our lives.*

By Anthony M. Coniaris

LIGHT & LIFE PUBLISHING
MINNEAPOLIS, MINNESOTA

Light & Life Publishing Company
P.O. Box 26421
Minneapolis, MN 55426-0421

Copyright © 2007
Light & Life Publishing Company

All rights reserved. No part of this book may be reproduced, stored in a retrieval system, or transmitted in any form or by any means, electronic, mechanical, photocopying, recording, or otherwise, without the written permission of Light & Life Publishing Company.

ISBN No.1-933654-05-8

THOUGHTS ON THE THEME

The unexamined life is not worth living.
—Socrates

He who knows his own sin is higher than the man who resurrects the dead by his prayers. He who has been granted the gift of seeing himself is superior to the man who sees the angels.
—St. Isaac the Syrian

Know yourselves ... He who knows himself, knows God.
—St. Anthony

We can never see the state of our soul in all its nakedness ...without the special grace and help of God, because the interior of our soul is always hidden from us by our self-love, prejudices, passions, worldly cares, delusions.
—St. Innocent of Alaska,
Indication of the Way into the Kingdom of Heaven

It is the greatest of all sciences to know one's self. For whoever knows one's self will know God; and in knowing God, will become like God.
—St. Clement of Alexandria

That you may acquaint yourself with God, first become acquainted with yourself.
—St. Cyprian of Carthage

We visit others as a matter of social obligation. How long has it been since we visited ourselves?
—Morris Adler

Only to man Thou hast made known Thy wayes, Of all the creatures both in sea and land. And put the pen alone into his hand, And made him secretarie of Thy praise.

—George Herbert, *The Temple*

TABLE OF CONTENTS

- How Difficult It Is to Know Oneself 1
- The Most Unexplored Territory: Self 8
- To Thine Own Self Be True 13
- Man's Infinite Capacity for Self-Deception 21
- Knowing Ourselves Through Relationships 35
- Finding One's True Self in God (Part One) 50
- Finding One's True Self in God (Part Two) 65
- Finding One's True Self Through Self-Examination . . .80
- Finding One's True Self Through Inner Stillness 93
- Finding One's True Self Through the Holy Spirit 100
- Finding One's True Self Through Humility 106
- Finding One's True Self Through
  Repentance and the Renunciation of Evil 112
- Finding One's True Self By Renouncing Pride 120

Chapter One

HOW DIFFICULT IT IS TO KNOW ONESELF

Beasts will bear witness to the faith…(but) in truth the most difficult of sciences is to know one's self. Not only our eye, from which nothing outside us escapes, cannot see itself, but our mind, so piercing to discover the sins of others, is slow to recognize its own faults. Thus my speech, after eagerly investigating what is external to myself, is slow and hesitating in exploring my own nature. Yet the beholding of heaven and earth does not make us know God better than the attentive study of our being does. I am, says the Prophet (Psalm 139:14), fearfully and wonderfully made: that is to say, in observing myself I have known Thy infinite wisdom.

—St. Basil the Great (329-379)

— Chapter One —

HOW DIFFICULT IT IS TO KNOW ONESELF

One of the most difficult things in life is to see ourselves as we truly are.

When Frederick II, an 18th century king of Prussia, went on an inspection tour of a Berlin prison, he was greeted with the cries of prisoners, who fell on their knees and protested their unjust imprisonment. While listening to their pleas of innocence, Frederick's eye was caught by a solitary figure in the corner, a prisoner seemingly unconcerned with all the commotion.

> "Why are you here?" Frederick asked him.
> "Armed robbery, Your Majesty."
> "Were you guilty?" the king asked.
> "Oh, yes, indeed, Your Majesty.
> I entirely deserve my punishment."

At that, Frederick summoned the jailer. "Release this man at once," he said. "I will not have him kept in this prison where he will corrupt all the fine innocent people who occupy it."

There is another story of a prisoner who kept insisting to the prison chaplain that he was innocent. The inmate asked him to intercede in his behalf before the judge. The chaplain shared this with the warden who told him, "They're all innocent. This is why you're here: to help them admit their guilt to themselves and to God."

You may remember the cartoon character Ziggy. He was floating one day in a life raft with sharks all around him. He asked angrily, "What did I ever do to deserve this?" A loud voice boomed back at him from the black sky above, "You want a list?"

When asked why he wanted to kill God, Nietzsche, an atheist, replied, "Because He knows too much."

THE EASIEST PERSON TO DECEIVE

One of our greatest difficulties in life is in being honest with ourselves. "To thine own self be true," (Shakespeare). Easier said than done! Sin, which blinds, has placed within us a tremendous capacity for self-deception. Demosthenes once said, "The easiest person to deceive is one's self."

Blessed Augustine said once that "the human heart is an abyss ... man is a vast deep ... the hairs on his head are easier by far to number than are his feelings, and the movements of his heart." Augustine goes on to say that man is unknown to himself, and still more unknown to anyone else: "In the sojourning of this carnal life each one carries his own heart, and every heart is closed to every other heart." "The heart is deep" (Psalm 63:6). What is needed more than anything else is a deeper knowledge of self: "Know thyself".

Knowing one's self is difficult because we are experts in manufacturing cover-ups to justify our shortcomings. We see this in the person who exhibits an eating disorder and denies that there is a problem; we see it in the person who exhibits a strong dependency on alcohol yet says drinking is just a way of relaxing from the stresses of the office; we see it in the person who uses cocaine and laughs at reports about how deadly the drug is; we see it in the woman who is unfaithful to her husband and sees nothing wrong with it. In fact, she justifies it by boasting that the adulterous relationship has actually improved her marriage! I meet people every day who seldom ever come to church or receive Communion or read the Bible or pray, who tell me that if they were to die today they are certain they would go straight to heaven. "...the folly of fools is deception" (Prov. 14:8).

Fr. John Garvey, an Antiochian priest and noted author, emphasized this when he wrote,

> *What worries me...is the capacity we all have for astonishing depths of self-deception. There may be some very rare people who believe themselves to be sincerely duplicitous and hypocritical, but I haven't met them. I don't know many people who believe themselves to be anything other than absolutely right on any point which matters deeply to them. Our attachment to our ideas fills emotional needs which often have nothing to do with the ideas themselves, and we are in danger when we deny this.**

THE WAY SIN BLINDS US

This tremendous capacity for self-deception is nothing new. It is the way sin has blinded us from the very beginning when Satan tempted Eve by telling her that if she disobeyed God, her eyes would be opened and she would become like God. The Bible warns against self-deception when it says, *The way of a fool is wise in his own eyes, but a wise man listens to advice* (Proverbs 12:15). Abba Poemen said, "The wickedness of men is hidden behind their backs." Blaise Pascal adds, "We run heedlessly into the abyss after putting something in front of us to stop us from seeing it (the abyss)." To use medical language, anyone who finds no fault in himself desperately needs a second opinion. And God provided this "second opinion" when

---

* *Against The Current.* John Garvey, Templegate Publishers, Springfiefld, IL. 2005

He gave us the Sacrament of Confession together with our spiritual Fathers and Mothers, for no person should ever be the judge in one's own case. "He who has himself as a mentor has a fool as a counselor," said one of the Desert Fathers.

EXAMPLES FROM THE BIBLE

The Bible recognizes the danger that self-deception poses for the life of faith and it offers many examples.

Peter, for example, told himself and others that he was strong, brave, courageous, and would never desert his Master even if all the others did. Yet, he denied Jesus three times. Was this not self-deception?

Was not the Pharisee self-deceived? He could see the Publican's sins but not his own.

When David stole another man's wife and had her husband killed so he could marry her, he felt no guilt. He was self-deceived. He probably said to himself, "I love Bathsheba so much that it doesn't matter what the rules say"; or "Our love is different, holy and pure"; or, "My love for Bathsheba hasn't violated her marriage because the marriage was already dead. Why else would she have consented to the affair?" David was self-deceived. He was not honest with himself. Satan had blinded him.

God had to send the prophet Nathan to prick David's conscience and bring him to an awareness of the two great sins he had committed: adultery and murder (2 Samuel 12:1-15). Ultimately David repented and confessed his wrongdoing in one of the greatest psalms ever written, Psalm 51:

— Chapter One —

> *Be merciful to me, O God, because of Your constant love...wipe away my sin.... I have sinned against You— only against You—and done what You consider evil. So You are right in judging me. I have been evil from the day I was born...Wash me and I shall be whiter than snow...Create a pure heart in me, O God, and put a new and loyal spirit in me.*

The prayer of the Publican, *Lord, be merciful to me the sinner,* is but a one-sentence summary of Psalm 51, one of the greatest expressions of sorrow over sin ever written.

THE APOSTLE JOHN ON SELF-DECEPTION

The Apostle John writes specifically about the danger of self-deception: *If we say we have no sin, we deceive ourselves, and the truth is not in us (1 John 1:8).* Could anyone have said it any better? This was the condition of Eve and Peter and David and the Pharisee. And it becomes our condition when we allow sin to blind us.

It is from this condition of self-deception and blindness that God in Christ came to deliver us. As God sent Nathan to prick David's conscience, so He sent Jesus to quicken us and to say to us, "You are the Pharisee who sees everyone else's sins but your own. Instead of pointing the finger at others and thinking that you are so much better than they are, you need to imitate the publican's humility and pray with him, *Lord, be merciful to me the sinner.*

"IF WE CONFESS OUR SINS..."

If we confess our sins, continues the Apostle John, *He (God) is faithful and just, and will forgive our sins and cleanse us from* all unrighteousness (1 John 1-9). But God cannot do this if we refuse to be honest with ourselves in our self-deceit.

"If anyone could see his own vices accurately without the veil of self-love, he would worry about nothing else in life" (St. John Climacus).

It is no exaggeration to say that the best lines of the gospel stories belong to sinners, but to sinners who don't hide their sins behind elaborate excuses; sinners who see themselves as they truly are, and, like the Publican, fall humbly to their knees before the Savior begging His mercy. "He went home"—said Jesus—"justified", forgiven, cleansed, with the joy of God's salvation in his heart. And so can we if we stop blaming others, see ourselves as we truly are, accept responsibility for ourselves, and confess our sins. God will not only "cleanse us from our unrighteousness" but will also give us a deeper insight into ourselves.

Someone once asked a pastor, "Are we going to know each other when we get to heaven?" The pastor wisely replied, "We won't know each other *until* we get to heaven."

How true! We wear so many masks in this life that it is hard to really get to know ourselves or others. We hide or rationalize so many bad things about ourselves. The tragedy is compounded by the fact that we hide also some of the beautiful things about ourselves. For example, we may feel a strong love for a spouse, a child, or a friend, but we find it difficult to express our feelings. So, we withhold our love. We hide what is most precious to us: our love for others. Thus, our spouse or children go through life deprived of knowing that they are loved. And without loving relationships they will never come to know who they are.

Chapter Two

THE MOST UNEXPLORED TERRITORY: SELF

The most unexplored territory in the world is self. Man is an enigma to himself.

The most difficult thing in life is knowledge of yourself.
—Thales

Man cannot stand too much reality.
—T.S. Eliot

Nothing can be closer to you than yourself. Yet it is amazing that you can know other things better than you know yourself. If you are holding an object in your hand and start to look for it, you will make others laugh. What is more at hand than your own soul? How can it know anything better than it knows itself?
—Guigo 1: Meditations

THE MOST UNEXPLORED TERRITORY: SELF

There is a story of a man who went to see his psychiatrist for help with his depression. The psychiatrist told him to cut back his 14-hour workday to eight hours, to go back home and spend his evenings in his study, quiet and alone. So the man tried it. He went back, read some of his favorite books, listened to classical music, watched some television and relaxed. After some weeks of this, he returned to his psychiatrist, complaining that he could see no improvement. On learning how the man had spent his time, the psychiatrist said, "But you didn't understand. I didn't want you to be with your favorite authors, or to listen to music or watch television. I wanted you to be alone with yourself." The man looked terrified and said, "I can't think of any worse company." The psychiatrist replied, "Yet this is the self you inflict on other people fourteen hours a day."

We hear much today about the importance of being yourself. But it is no good being yourself if "being yourself" provides you with bad company and brings you into collision with other people. We live with our self every day—and, if it's a bad self, it's a self that inflicts pain on others: spouse, children, friends. Hence, it is not only important but mandatory that we come to know our true self, the authentic self, the image of God in us. "The unexamined life is not worth living," said Socrates.

MAN: AN ENIGMA TO HIMSELF

The most unexplored territory in the world is self. Man, who has explored not only the surface of the earth but its very depths; man who has explored outer space and landed on the moon, this same man remains an enigma to himself. He has

— Chapter Two —

learned to control lightning, steam, wind, electricity. He has split the atom and harnessed its power, yet he remains an enigma to himself and is unable to control his own will and passions. That is why we may say without fear of exaggeration that the most unexplored of all territories is self.

Anthony de Mello tells the story of an elderly gentleman who ran a curio and antique shop in a large city. A tourist once stepped in and got to talking with the old man about the hundreds of items that were stacked in the shop.

The tourist asked, "What would you say is the strangest, the most mysterious thing you have here?"

The old man surveyed the hundreds of curios, antiques, stuffed animals, shrunken heads, mounted fish, birds, archaeological finds, deer heads, then turned to the tourist and said, "The strangest thing in this shop is unquestionably myself."

Dr. Armand Nicholi, Harvard professor of Psychiatry, would agree. He writes,

> *Within the university, students and professors scrutinize every possible aspect of our universe—from the billions of galaxies to subatomic particles, electrons, quarks—but they assiduously avoid examining their own lives. In the wider world, we keep hectically busy and fill every free moment of our day with some form of diversion—work, computers, television, movies, radio, magazines, newspapers, sports, alcohol, drugs, parties. Perhaps we distract ourselves because looking at our lives confronts us with our lack of meaning, our unhappiness, and our loneliness and with the difficulty,*

the fragility, and the unbelievable brevity of life...But until we examine our lives, we can do little to make them less unhappy and more fulfilling.*

It was to underline the importance of self-knowledge that Socrates said, "Know thyself", and it was for this reason that the wise men of ancient Greece inscribed these same words at the oracle of Delphi: "Know thyself".

You can't know anything at all if you do not know yourself (Guigo 1: Meditations).

THE IMPORTANCE OF SELF-KNOWLEDGE

The Church Fathers greatly emphasized the importance of self-knowledge. Isaac of Nineveh said, "He who sees himself as he truly is, is greater than one who can raise the dead." Commenting on this statement someone said that knowing oneself is raising the dead.

Isaac goes on to say, "When a man knows himself, the knowledge of all things is granted to him, for to know one's self is the fullness of the knowledge of all things."

The Desert Fathers emphasized the importance of self-knowledge without which we can neither rightly repent nor seek to amend our lives. They kept emphasizing over and over the importance of paying attention to oneself, guarding the mind and the heart, always highlighting the virtue of discernment, by which they meant the ability to diagnose what is going on in one's life at any moment, just as a spider senses the slightest movement of any insect on its web.

---

* *The Question of God*. Armand Nicholi. Simon and Schuster, New York, NY 2002.

– Chapter Two –

"MY SINS RUN OUT BEHIND ME"

An example of the keen self-knowledge of the Desert Fathers is the following story which is told of one of the abbas,

> *A brother at Scetis committed a fault. A council was called to which Abba Moses was invited, but he refused to go to it. Then the priest sent someone to say to him, "Come, for everyone is waiting for you." So he got up and went. He took a leaking jug filled with water and carried it with him. The others came out to meet him and said to him, "What is this, Father?" The old man said, "My sins run out behind me and I do not see them and today I am going to judge the sins of another." When they heard this, they said no more to the brother who was to be accused but forgave him.*

To know oneself is to gain understanding not only of oneself but also of others; it is to be more forgiving, more tolerant, more empathetic. Indeed, we need to confront ourselves regularly if we are to repent, amend our lives and grow in love to the fullness of the image of God, toward Theosis.

Harvard researcher Gordon Allport discovered this truth. He wrote, "Knowledge of oneself tends to be associated with tolerance for others. People who are self-aware, self-critical, are not given to the ponderous habit of passing blame to others for what is their own responsibility. They know their own capabilities and shortcomings."

Isaac of Nineveh extolled knowledge of self with these extravagant words, "The man who is deemed worthy to see himself is greater than he who is deemed worthy to see the angels."

Chapter Three

TO THINE OWN SELF BE TRUE

We visit others as a matter of social obligation. How long has it been since we visited with ourselves?
—Morris Adler

We are strangers to ourselves. That is the most painful part of being human.
—Henri Nouwen

People travel to wonder at the heights of mountains, at the huge waves of the sea, at the long courses of rivers, at the vast compass of the ocean, at the circular motion of the stars; and they pass by themselves without wondering.
—Saint Augustine

Chapter Three

TO THINE OWN SELF BE TRUE

Shakespeare had Polonius say in *Hamlet*, "To thine own self be true, and it must follow as the night the day, thou canst not be false to any man."

To know oneself, to be true to one's authentic self is a foundational principle that will affect everything we do in life.

St. Gregory Palamas considered self-knowledge greater than natural science or philosophy,

> *For a man to know God, and to know himself...is a knowledge superior to natural science and astronomy and to all philosophy.*

LOSING HALF OUR RESOURCES

Many people go through life knowing very little about themselves. For this reason they use only a tiny part of their resources. They surrender to timidity, skepticism, self-doubt and despair. As a result, great areas of strength remain dormant, undiscovered, underdeveloped. This is the terrible price we pay for lack of self-knowledge.

"I YAM WHAT I YAM"

Many people are like the famous cartoon character Popeye whose favorite expression was, "I yam what I yam." It was an expression he used often as an explanation for his shortcomings. It is a terrible expression because it doesn't give him much of a shot at being what he "yam not". "When it comes to me," he seemed to be saying, "Don't get your hopes too high. Don't expect too much. 'I yam what I yam.'"

This is the attitude that paralyzes people and prevents them from achieving their full potential in life. It is an attitude that is generated by lack of self-knowledge.

Jacob Boehme considered self-knowledge the "one necessary thing":

> *The best measure that a man can attain unto in this world is true knowledge; even the knowledge of himself; for man is the great mystery of God, the microcosm, or complete abridgement of the whole universe; he is …God's masterpiece, a living emblem and hieroglyphic of eternity and time; and therefore to know whence he is, and what his temporal and eternal well-being are, must needs be the one necessary thing, to which all our chief study should aim, and in comparison of which all the wealth of this world is but dross and a loss to us.*

"HOW ARE THINGS WHERE YOU LIVE?"

The following story illustrates a powerful truth about knowing one's self. A man from the West Coast considered moving to a town on the East Coast. He asked a local resident, "How are things in this town?" The resident said, "Well, how are things where you now live?" "Oh, just fine! The people are nice and friendly and the town is a fine place to live," was the response. The resident replied, "That is exactly what you will find in this town, nice, friendly people, a fine place to live."

Now, if the man considering the move had said, "The town I now live in is unpleasant and the people are rude and unfriendly," then the resident would have said, "That is the way this town is too, unpleasant, with rude and unfriendly people."

— Chapter Three —

If I move to get away from unpleasant people or unpleasant situations, I may in the new locality, with different neighbors, run into the same situations.

The lesson to be learned is this:

Until I meet and overcome a problem situated within myself,
    repent of it,
    learn from it,
    grow through it,
unless I come to know myself, I shall find myself facing essentially the same problem, perhaps in a slightly different shape and form, wherever I go. No matter where I go, the same self will travel with me. As the self is, so is the world around me. For, I will always be seeing the world through the same unreformed, distorted self.

A DIFFICULT TASK

Knowing one's self is not easily attained. It is a life-long task. The Greek philosopher Thales said, "The most difficult thing in life is knowledge of yourself." Benjamin Franklin agreed. He said once, "There are three things extremely hard: steel, a diamond, and to know one's self." Panayiotis Nellas, a Greek Orthodox theologian, believed that the mysterious character of the self is due to the fact that we are made in God's image. Since God is beyond understanding, His image, within us, says Dr. Nellas, is also uniquely incomprehensible. St. Macarius the Great of Egypt (300-390) described what a difficult and life-long process it is to get to know one's self. It seems he was ahead of his time in his discovery of "depth psychology". This is how he described man's journey into the inner depths of self:

> ...As when one peels an onion, one layer after another is removed, and the innermost core, out of which growth reaches up toward the light, lies revealed. In the same manner, that which arouses discontent in us, such as dissatisfaction, impatience, impetuosity, anger, envy, fear, anguish, anxiety, hate, dispiritedness, laziness, dejection, and doubt, one by one layer, must be shed off, before one reaches one's innermost chamber in one's heart. There in the innermost chamber, one will find in addition, a crawling serpent nestled in comfort. The serpent's name is <u>self love</u> and <u>self pity</u>.
>
> ...When you strive now to enter your innermost depths, you will be aware besides your own true face, that the crawling serpent has nestled there, and wounded your soul's most vital organ.
>
> ...If now you succeed to slay this serpent, you may pride yourself on your purity before God. But, be aware again, that the serpent, for the great, great majority of us, cannot be slain during this earthly life, it can only be made sluggish! Therefore, bow humbly, as a needy sinner, and pray to God about all that lurks within you....

We can see from these words of St. Macarius that the Church Fathers were accomplished professionals at exploring and mapping the mysterious inner psyche.

HE COULD NOT FIND HIMSELF

Anthony deMello tells the story of a person who was forgetful. Each morning when he woke he had such a hard time finding his clothes that he almost feared to go to bed when he thought of the trouble he would have on waking.

– Chapter Three –

One night he got himself a pencil and pad and jotted down the exact name and location of each item of clothing as he undressed. Next morning he pulled out his pad and read, "pants"—there they were. He stepped into them. "Shirt"—there it was. He pulled it over his head. "Hat"—there it was. He slapped it on his head.

He was very pleased about all this till a horrible thought struck him, "and I—where am I?" He had forgotten to jot that down. So he searched and searched, but in vain. He could not find himself.

This has always been man's great problem: ignorance of self which leads to all sorts of problems: identity crises, confusion, inner slavery. George Gurdjieff expressed this supremely well when he wrote these words,

> *The first reason for man's inner slavery is his ignorance, and above all, his ignorance of himself. Without self-knowledge...man cannot be free, he cannot govern himself and he will always remain a slave, and the plaything of forces acting upon him. This is why in all ancient teaching the first demand at the beginning of the way to liberation was: Know Thyself.*

Knowing who we are and, above all, whose we are, is the starting point of a journey that can lead us to become through Christ "partakers of divine nature". I.M. Kontzevich describes this inner journey when he writes,

> *The way to God leads through knowledge of oneself. "No one can know God without knowing himself," repeats St. Athanasius the Great after St. Anthony the Great... Usually people suffer from blindness and self-delusion*

and are unable to see their fallen state. Therefore, becoming aware of one's own true state and of evil within oneself is the first step toward knowledge of onself.*

A PERSONAL, PRIVATE REVOLUTION

When Muslims make their pilgrimage to Mecca, they engage in a ceremony during which they throw stones at a building representing the devil. Yet the devil—evil—resides not outside oneself but within. And unless one comes to know this, one will never come to true self knowledge. Archimandrite Sophrony said once that "the only revolution we should be thinking about is a personal, private moral one." It is not the devil who is to blame; it is not the devil who pulls the strings. He can only suggest or tempt. We have the final say. The revolution for a better world begins within with self-knowledge, with honest acknowledgement of one's sinful self.

It is because of ignorance of self that man is fragmented within. Thomas Merton expressed this in a classic statement: "Man is not at peace with his fellow man because he is not at peace with himself; he is not at peace with himself, because he is not at peace with God."

"MY NAME IS LEGION"

The fragmented personality is illustrated powerfully in the encounter of Jesus with the demoniac (Mark 5:1-13). When Jesus asked him, "What is thy name?", he answered, "My name is Legion for we are many." This unclean spirit was in reality many unclean spirits who had taken over this man's personality. Commenting on this encounter, Fr. Pavel Florensky writes,

---

* I.M. Kontzevich. Translated by Olga Kohansky. *The Acquisition of the Holy Spirit in Ancient Russia.* St. Herman of Alaska Press, Platina, CA. 1988.

"This precisely is the general type of the expulsion of unclean spirits. The prayer of exorcism by the Lord's name forces an illusory person to fall apart into fractions, into a 'legion' of demonic states, each of which passes itself off as a person."* The demoniac was a civil war of conflicting selves. Jesus restored him to wholeness, to his true self.

THE LONGEST JOURNEY

The longest journey is the journey inward," wrote Dag Hammarskjold. It is a long and difficult journey—this journey to self-knowledge. Yet it is, of all journeys, most important. The Church Fathers emphasize that it is *within* that we will find the Kingdom of God. The greatest resource we have is within and the greatest enemy we have is within. That is why knowledge of self is so crucial. Without knowledge of self one cannot govern one's self and will always remain a slave.

---

* *The Pillar and Ground of Truth.* Pavel Florensky. Princeton Univ. Press, Princeton, NJ.

Chapter Four

MAN'S INFINITE CAPACITY FOR SELF-DECEPTION

Defense mechanisms can be described biblically as flesh-patterns. They are ways by which our lower nature—the "flesh"—resists the truth about ourselves, favoring lies and illusions.

The heart is deceitful above all things .

—Jeremiah 17:9

— Chapter Four —

EGO DEFENSES

What makes it even more difficult to know one's true self is that "the serpent who dwells in the innermost chamber of the heart" (St. Macarius) is the father of lies. He comes up with a bag full of tricks to prevent us from seeing and knowing ourselves. Psychologists call these "tricks" defense mechanisms or ego defenses. Whether we call them alibis, evasions, denial, rationalization, projection, repression, their main purpose is to prevent us from seeing ourselves by denying our faults, projecting them on to others, or devising excuses for them. Their purpose is to blind us to our real self, preventing us from accepting responsibility, repenting, and moving on to growth and progress in Christ (Christification).

Not caring to see our true selves, we waste immense amounts of energy endeavoring to hide or deny the truth. "The truth will make you free", said Jesus. Indeed it will, but first it may make us miserable with what we discover in ourselves. Yet that misery, that disgust is designed to lead us not to despondency but to God's infinite mercy, forgiveness, and newness of life.

SELF-JUSTIFICATION THROUGH RATIONALIZATION

John Powell describes one of the common forms of ego defense: rationalization,

> *The most common form of ego defense is "rationalization". As a technique for self-justification, it is hard to beat. We find some reason for our action which justifies it. We "think" (rationalize) our way to a pre-ordained conclusion. Very often there are two reasons for*

everything we do: the alleged good reason and the real reason. Rationalization is not only self-deceit but eventually corrupts all sense of integrity....

As with all ego defense mechanisms, there is always something which I cannot admit in myself, something that I would like to do which appears wrong, or something that would make me feel better if I could believe it. Rationalization is the bridge which makes my wishes the facts. It is the use of intelligence to deny the truth; it makes us dishonest with ourselves, and, if we cannot be honest with ourselves, we certainly cannot be honest with anyone else. It consequently sabotages all human authenticity. It disintegrates and fragments the personality.*

Such ego defense mechanisms can be described biblically as flesh-patterns. They are the ways our lower nature—the flesh—resists the truth about ourselves, favoring lies and illusions.

Fully aware of all these ego defenses, Augustine called on us to avoid what he called "the lust of vindicating ourselves". To prevent people who knew him as a bishop from having an overly exalted view of him, Augustine wrote his famous *Confessions*. St. Paul did the same when he was forced to brag about his credentials to the Corinthians. He made sure he ended with the acknowledgment of a humiliating weakness (2 Cor. 11:22-30).

MASKS

In addition to all the defense mechanisms, or more accurately, ego defenses, another factor that makes it difficult for us to

* *"Why Am I Afraid to Tell You Who I Am?"* John Powell. Argus Communications, Chicago, IL. 1969.

— Chapter Four —

come to know ourselves is that we do not *want* to know ourselves. We are constantly trying to create our own version of ourselves different from the one we are. Some of us have become a bundle of selves, a "legion" of selves, all false selves claiming to be the real self.

We are like the ancient Greek actors who carried a portable mask to cover their faces when they were impersonating someone. The mask was called *prosopeion* which was used to cover the *prosopon*, or face, which is the real, true person. This is what we call hypocrisy: to pretend to be what one is not; the refusal to be ourselves. Many people do this by defining themselves by what they *have* rather than by what they *are*. Possession of things becomes the ultimate criterion of personhood. It could be the possession of wealth, power, fame, etc. Thus, self, personhood, comes to depend entirely on externals.

Metropolitan Anthony Bloom says that many people wear a mask even when they come before God in prayer. He writes that when praying many people "put forward someone who is not our real self, who is an actor, a sham, a stage personality," when what we need is to pray a simple prayer, "Help me, O God, to put off all pretenses and to find my true self."*

The Psalmist realized his need for God's help in knowing himself when he wrote this beautiful prayer:

> *O Lord, You have searched me and known me.*
> *You know my sitting down and my rising up;*
> *You understand my thought afar off.*
> *You comprehend my path and my lying down,*

---

* *Living Prayer*. Anthony Bloom. Templegate Publ., Springfield, IL. 1966.

And are acquainted with all my ways.
For there is not a word on my tongue
But behold, O Lord, You know it altogether.
You have hedged me behind and before,
And laid Your hand upon me.
Such knowledge is too wonderful for me;
It is high, I cannot attain it.
(Psalm 139:1-6)

Dr. Hans Selye was one of the world's greatest authorities on stress. He discovered that one of the greatest sources of stress is the fact that people try to be what they are not. He explained,

> No animal is guilty of this, but you see it everywhere in our society. The woman of fifty who tries to look and act as if she were twenty-five. The insecure businessman who poses as a great expert in his field when actually his knowledge is quite limited. The individual who puts on a great show of piety when his private life is full of dishonesty. Jesus likened such hypocrites, you remember, to whitewashed tombs, clean and shining on the outside, but full of rottenness within.

REPENTANCE AND CONFESSION LEAD TO SELF-KNOWLEDGE

The Russian word for freedom indicates that we are called to be our own selves, not to imitate or ape others, but to be ourselves in the image of the One Who is perfect freedom and perfect love—truly Himself: Christ.

How can we remove the masks we wear to discover our true self? Fr. John Chryssavgis offers this sage advice:

Chapter Four

> *When I can confess my peculiarity, my brokenness to someone who does not shame me, who will stand as a representative of the community and as a witness before God, then my healing can begin. When I take off the mask, and—together with at least one other person—look clearly at my vulnerability, then my recovery and restoration has begun.**

This requires honesty, humility and a trusted spiritual mentor. One cannot do it alone. Dorotheos writes, "Being passionate, we should absolutely not trust ourselves to our own heart; for a crooked rule makes crooked even that which is straight."

The purpose of repentance and confession is to clear away the false masks that we may discover the true God-given self, the image of God in us. Bishop Ware writes,

> *It (repentance) is not despondency but eager expectation; it is not to feel that one has reached an impasse, but to take the way out. It is not self-hatred but the affirmation of my true self as made in God's image. To repent is to look, not downward at my own shortcomings, but upward at God's love; not backward with self-reproach, but forward with trustfulness. It is to see, not what I have failed to be, but what by the grace of Christ I can yet become.***

The purpose of repentance and confession is to help us find our true self in God, just as the prodigal found his true self when he returned to the father.

> *Sever me from myself that I may be grateful to you;*
> *May I perish to myself that I may be safe in you;*

---

* *Soul Mending: the Art of Spiritual Direction.* John Chryssavgis. HCO Press, Brookline, MA. 2000.
** *"The Orthodox Experience of Repentance".* Sobornost. Vol. 2, Number 1. 1980.

May I die to myself that I may live in you;
May I wither to myself that I may blossom in you;
May I be emptied of myself that I may be filled with You;
May I be nothing to myself that I may be all to you.
Amen.
–Desiderius Erasmus

Fr. Maximos of Mount Athos considers confession a valuable aid for self-knowledge. He says,

> Confession is nothing but a method to help us take a good look at our real self. Like drug addicts who need their doses, we construct false images and idols of ourselves. Confession brings us to the truth about who we are, but in a philanthropic manner, for the sake of our salvation. Anyway, that is what I try to do when I offer confession to people.
>
> It is easier for people like tax collectors, prostitutes, and sinners to find God than those considered to be moral and religiously correct. These people have no idols of themselves. They are a total failure and disaster to themselves and they know it. But God has the power to reassemble them once they have been torn apart. That can happen, of course, only if they marshal the power to hand over the pieces to God in order to allow him to put them back together. Believe me, the pieces of the tax collector and the prostitute are much more valuable than the idol of the individual who is proud of his religious virtues.*

---

* *Gifts of the Desert.* Kyriacos C. Markides. Doubleday. A Division of the Random House, New York, NY. 2005

— Chapter Four —

DO NOT DESCEND INTO THE DEPTHS OF SELF ALONE

"God can save the sinner we are; he cannot save the saint we are not," said Metropolitan Anthony Bloom. To discover the sinner we are, we need to descend into the depths of the self—but never alone. There is only one person who dares to go down with me to the depths of my sinful self—and that is the Lord Jesus. The Church Fathers warn us that it is dangerous to descend into one's depths alone—without prayer and a spiritual mentor. The purpose of the downward descent through self-examination and repentance is an upward ascent through the discovery of the true self in the image of God and the subsequent journey to Christification and theosis. We *descend* in order to *ascend*.

We cannot come to know our sins unless we draw near to the all-Pure One. The Abbot Mathois said once, "The nearer a man approaches to God, the greater sinner he sees himself to be." The Prophet Isaiah saw God, and said that he was unclean and undone (Isaiah 6:1-3).

We cannot come to know ourselves truly without God. Repentance is not attained solely by our own effort. It is equally a gift of the Holy Spirit.

SOME AMAZING RATIONALIZATIONS

Human beings are amazingly skillful in rationalizing the most perverse kinds of behavior imaginable. Over the years I have heard or read unbelievable justifications; justifications for the sexual abuse of children by their parents; justifications for adultery; justifications for homosexuality; justifications for practicing sado-masochism. When it comes to sin, human beings are capable of the most demonically outlandish uses of rationalization in order to make what they want to do *seem* perfectly appropriate. Dostoevsky had a profound insight into the human soul when he wrote, "The devil struggles with God and the field of battle is the human heart."

One of the strangest rationalizations I have encountered is the excuse Gypsies use for stealing. They rationalize stealing by telling the following story. Supposedly, a Gypsy was in the crowd that followed Jesus to Golgotha. He tried to steal the nails from the Roman soldier who was to nail Jesus to the cross. The Gypsy was able to steal only one nail, the extra long one that was meant for Jesus' head or heart. The soldier suspected the Gypsy, and beat him ferociously to make him tell where the nail was. But to no avail. Greatly appreciative, Jesus then told the Gypsy from the cross that from then on Gypsies had the right to wander the earth and steal. This is how far some people will go to rationalize sinful behavior!

In 1991 a Gallup poll showed that 78 per cent of Americans expected to go to heaven when they die. However, many of them hardly ever prayed, read the Bible, or attended church. They admitted that they lived to please only themselves, not God. Is not this part of what the Bible calls "the deceitfulness of sin"? It is for this reason that Jesus will say at the Last Judgment to some who will claim to be His disciples, "Depart from me. I never knew you."

THE ALCOHOLIC AND DENIAL

A very sad example of such deception is found in the alcoholic. Practically all alcoholics are addicted to lying. An alcoholic will

Chapter Four

seldom ever admit he is an alcoholic. He may admit to his excessive drinking or drunkenness, but not to alcoholism. Denial is a major symptom of alcoholism. Yet those who have studied alcoholism tell us not to be too quick in condemning the alcoholic as a liar. Why? Because studies have shown that the alcoholic has truly lost the ability to see himself as he truly is. He is totally blind to himself. This is because chemically induced blackouts cause a complete loss of memory. This is why Jesus warned that sin blinds, just as it blinded David to his sins of adultery and murder until God sent Nathan to open his eyes. Perhaps this is what caused someone to say, "Maturity consists in no longer being taken in by yourself."

AN INFINITE CAPACITY FOR SELF DECEPTION

We have an infinite capacity for self-deception. Demosthenes said once, "The easiest thing of all is to deceive one's self; for what a man wishes, he generally believes to be true." "Nature didn't make us perfect," someone said, "but at least she had the kindness to make us blind to our faults."

How easily is man deceived. This is why the author of the book of Hebrews warns, "That none of you be hardened by the deceitfulness of sin" (Hebrews 3:13). Persisted in and rationalized, sin blinds us to ourselves and blunts our conscience. "If we say that we have no sin, we deceive ourselves, and the truth is not in us" (1 John 1:8). "The heart is devious above all else; it is perverse—who can understand it? I the Lord test the mind and search the heart, to give to all according to their ways, according to the fruit of their doing" (Jer. 17:9-10).

"All deceit begins in self-deceit" (*Theologica Germanica*). No decent, self-respecting person can lie to others without first lying to himself. Of all forms of deception, self-deception is the most deadly, and of all deceived persons, the self-deceived are least likely to discover the fraud. They live in illusion, in a fantasy world of their own and are so blinded that they actually relish their illusions.

People can con their consciences and excuse themselves for anything. One student who was found cheating rationalized his behavior by saying that he had such a horrendous headache, the professor was such a bore, the test was so unfair, and his parents were nagging him so relentlessly to get good grades that he not only had a right to cheat, he had a solemn obligation!

LIES: ONE OF THE ROOTS OF MENTAL ILLNESS

Psychiatrists tell us that invariably one of the root causes of mental illness is an interlocking system of lies we have been told and lies we have told ourselves. For healing to occur these lies need to be uncovered in an atmosphere of utter honesty and contrition. Hence, for self-knowledge to occur repentance and confession are essential.

Jesus explained why people build up ego defenses when He said that they love darkness rather than light. They flee the light to hide in the darkness because their actions are sinful (John 3:19). They not only flee from the light; they despise it, preferring their own blindness as well as the delusions that blindness creates. All this explains why it is so difficult to know one's self that St. John Climacus once said, "If anyone could

Chapter Four

see his own vices accurately without the veil of self-love, he would worry about nothing else in his life."

> *Our self-will is so subtle and so deeply rooted within us, so covered with excuses and defended by false reasoning that it seems to be a demon. When we cannot do our own will in one way, we do it in another, under all kinds of pretexts.*
> –Catherine of Genoa (1447-1510)

The words of Jesus in this respect are clear. He tells us, in paraphrase, that he who seeks only his false self brings his true self to ruin; whereas he who unmasks his false self and brings it to naught for me discovers who he truly is, i.e., the image of God. "You were darkness once, but now you are light in the Lord.... Try to discover what the Lord wants of you" (Eph. 5:8-14).

One of the first demands the Lord Jesus makes on us is that we be honest with ourselves, that we sweep everything false and pretentious out of our lives and build our whole existence on truth. When we speak of conversion what else do we mean but that a person has come to honest terms with himself and God. He had been living falsely, but now through the grace of God he has had an awakening; he sees himself as he really is, and life as it truly is, and God as He is. This is the beginning of salvation; but it is also the beginning of healing for man's spirit. One of the main purposes of psychiatry, for example, is to try to get a person to strip himself naked of all excuses and rationalizations—all the layers of self-deceit—that he may begin to build his life on the truth about himself. "O Lord, Thou desirest truth in the inward parts," says the Psalmist. "You shall know the truth and the truth shall set you free," said

Jesus. To know the truth is to know not only our failures and sins; it is to know also God's great love in Christ Jesus which accepts us and forgives us, no matter what our sin, and helps us rise above it—all the way to union with Him (*Theosis*).

Dr. Kenneth L. Bakken, a physician as well as an ordained pastor, provided an excellent conclusion to this chapter when he wrote in his very insightful book *The Journey into God*:

> *Jesus calls us on the Way—a journey that may, in fact, cost us everything, including our lives. It requires of us the death of the false self. The false or ego self refers to the manner in which we usually describe or understand ourselves—personality, personal and cultural history, beliefs, attitudes, and relationships. Thomas Merton writes, "We have the choice of two identities: the external mask which seems to be real and which lives by a shadowy autonomy for the brief moment of earthly existence, and the hidden inner person who seems to us to be nothing, but who can give himself externally to the truth in whom he subsists." The ego self is who and what the world tells us we are; it wears the mask. It perpetuates the myth of our essential separateness, which sets us against one another. It is the self we protect with psychological defenses and rigid patterns of behavior. It is the self—individual and corporate—that we seek to preserve through acts of emotional, spiritual, and physical violence.*
>
> *Baptism is a training in dying and sets us on the course of the discipleship of the cross. "For as we participate in Christ's dying and rising, we die to our old selves and find a future not bound by the past. The focus of this dying and rising is the Christian practice of baptism, and it also*

– Chapter Four –

involves a lifelong practice of living into that baptism, of daily dying to old selves and living into the promise of an embodied new life."*

---

* *The Journey into God.* Kenneth L. Bakken. Augsburg Publ. Co., Mpls, MN. 2000.

Chapter Five

KNOWING OURSELVES THROUGH RELATIONSHIPS

One of the main methods God uses to enable us to see ourselves is other people.

Everything that irritates us about others can lead us to an understanding of ourselves.
—Karl Jung

For if anyone is a hearer of the word and not a doer, he is like a man observing his natural face in a mirror; for he observes himself, goes away, and immediately forgets what kind of man he was.
—James 1:23-24

Even the Persons of the Trinity exist in the relationship. One learns that it is in loving others, and in being loved, that the truest self emerges.
—A.M.C

― Chapter Five ―

SELF-KNOWLEDGE IS RELATIONAL

Dr. Chrestos Yannaras emphasizes that self-knowledge is relational. He writes: "The Greek word for person *prosopon*, has the literal meaning 'face': each of us is authentically a person only insofar as he or she 'faces' others and relates to them in love." Fr. Dumitru Staniloae teaches the same when he writes, "I do not know myself apart from a relationship with others.... For myself, insofar as I am not loved, I am incomprehensible." Thus, for both Staniloae and Yannaras, self-knowledge is not only relational; it also involves love. In other words, we come to know ourselves by participating in loving relationships with persons. Dialogue in a communion of love is a prerequisite for self-knowledge.

This is what happens in marriage. One husband wrote:

> *I suppose we all have blind spots, faults that we don't see. I didn't know what mine were before I was married, but after sharing life with Carol for five years I can easily list them.*
>
> *When I do the dishes, I leave one pot or pan in the sink unwashed. When I'm engrossed in a book, speaking to me is like talking to a brick wall. I always forget to close the closet door, I always pick up just the section of the newspaper Carol wants to read and I never put my dirty socks in the dirty clothes bag. On the other hand, Carol never cleans the bathtub, she has no sense of direction, she hates to lose an argument and she can't cook a hamburger patty. What amuses us both is that we weren't aware of any of these shortcomings before we were married. It was only after living together....*

Now a cynic might see this as a good argument against marriage. On the contrary, I see it as a good argument for it. Otherwise, how would I know the full depth of God's forgiveness (and my wife's)? Maybe that's why God wants us to be Christians together, in churches, in prayer, in friendship—you can't be a Christian alone.

Self-knowledge requires loving relationships. To know our true self is to know that we are loved by God beyond all measure.

THE SAMARITAN WOMAN FINDS HERSELF IN CHRIST

We see an example of this in the encounter of Jesus with the Samaritan woman (John 4:5-26). After talking theoretically about where God is to be worshiped, Jesus stabs her awake with a very personal question, "Go, call your husband and bring him here." William Barclay comments, "The woman stiffened as if a sudden pain had caught her; she recoiled as if hit by a sudden shock; she grew white as one who had seen a sudden apparition; and so indeed she had, for she had suddenly caught sight of herself. She was suddenly compelled to face herself and the looseness and the immorality ... of her life.... No man ever sees himself as he really is until he sees himself in the presence of Christ; and then he is appalled at the sight of himself. There is another way of putting it—Christianity begins with a sense of sin."*

A JOURNEY OF RISING AND FALLING

Christianity may begin with a sense of sin but it does not end there. The sense of sin marks the beginning of a journey that

---
* *The Gospel of John*. Wm. Barclay. Vol. 1. Westminster Press, Louisville, KY. 1956.

leads to Christification and theosis. C.S. Lewis described the Christian life as a journey of rising and falling:

> *No amount of falls will really undo us if we keep on picking ourselves up each time. We shall of course be very muddy and tattered children by the time we reach home. But the bathrooms are all ready, the towels put out, and the clean clothes in the airing cupboard. The only fatal thing is to lose one's temper and give it up. It is when we notice the dirt that God is most present in us: It is the very sign of His presence.*

If you entered a dimly lit room, the place would probably look fairly clean. But if you installed a hundred bulbs of a thousand watts each, you would put the whole room under a magnifying glass. You would probably see all kinds of strange and wonderful little creatures that might make you think twice about staying in that room. This is what happened to the Samaritan woman when she encountered Christ. The "dirt" was suddenly revealed, but be of good cheer; Jesus tells us that "the shower is ready, the towels are put out and the clean clothes are waiting for us" in the closet of His grace.

METAMORPHOSED INTO AN APOSTLE

Christianity begins with a sense of sin but does not end there. Jesus holds up a mirror before the Samaritan woman; she sees her real self. But in addition to a mirror, He holds up before her an icon of who she truly is, having been created in the image of God. His purpose is to heal and restore her to her true self as the image of God. And she emerges, metamorphosed—"morphed" as they say—into a new person. She becomes an apostle, bringing the gospel to those in her village. "Come, see a Man who told me all things that I ever did. Could this be the

Christ?.... and many of the Samaritans of that city believed in Him because of the word of the woman who testified, 'He told me all that I ever did'" (John 4:29-39).

MORPHED INTO A NEW SELF

This is what happens when we encounter Jesus. The old false self morphs into the new self, the real self of the image of God in us. When this morphing happens we find ourselves *wanting* to do the things Jesus would have done. We become new persons. We discover our true selves in Christ Jesus. We are "Christified" as St. Paul says, "I live, yet not I, but Christ who lives in me."

Ellen Charry explains the theology behind this experience when she writes,

> *Growth in the spiritual life is advancing self-discovery and realization of the godly identity that is ours by virtue of God's having made us for himself and after His image.... This is our true identity, "true" in the sense of 'best'.**

SELF-KNOWLEDGE THROUGH INTERVENTION

An innovative way of helping loved ones with addictions come to realize how critical their situation is, is called *intervention*. If a person is an alcoholic, for example, the family does not wait for the addicted one to hit bottom and cause untold damage along the way before he/she comes to himself. What do they do? They intervene.

* *Theology Today.* October 2004.

– Chapter Five –

Let us use the example of a woman who was married to an alcoholic. The husband thought he could "hold his liquor", but he was continually making a humiliating spectacle of himself. So one day his wife, without his knowledge, took some pictures of him while he was dead drunk. A few days later she laid them next to her husband's plate at breakfast. Seeing them was a revelation to him. He could no longer deny the truth of his condition. How many of us there are who, if we could only get one real honest view of ourselves, would forever change the course of our lives. But for this to happen we need God and we need people, people who love, people who care, people who are willing to intervene in love in order to reflect the truth back to us.

"ANOTHER BEARS WITNESS ABOUT ME"

"I do not know myself apart from a relationship with others," said Fr. D. Staniloae. When Jesus was asked for evidence that his claims were true, He said, "If I bear witness about myself, my witness need not be accepted as true; but it is Another who is bearing witness about me, and I know that the witness which He bears is true" (John 5:31). Jesus was playing by the rules of the Jewish people. These rules taught that the unsupported testimony of one person cannot be taken as proof. Before a thing can be considered proven, there must be evidence from at least two or three other persons. Who were the "others" who bore witness to Jesus as the Son of God? They were God the Father as well as the miracles He performed (John 5:31-36).

Self-knowledge is relational. We cannot know ourselves without the testimony of others. That is why God established the Church, that we may live in a community of faith. Robert Burns said once, "Would that some power would give us the gift of seeing ourselves as others see us." That "power" is God. The gift of seeing ourselves as we are comes from the Holy Spirit and from the other members of the body, the Church. The wisdom of the Church and Scripture is that we are never saved alone. We are meant to get in touch with ourselves in the midst of a community of faith, the body of Christ.

Dr. Kenneth L. Bakken brings this out in his excellent book *The Journey into God*:

> *Our true being as a person, as opposed to our false self as an individual, only comes into existence when we are in living communion with God. The actual translation from the book of Leviticus in the Torah is "you shall love your neighbor as being your own self." Your neighbor is your true self. This love (agape) is an expression of the Holy Spirit. We must recognize our essential communion (koinonia): there is no true self except the one that comes into being by the act of love and self-emptying. It is only by loving the other that "myself" actually emerges. In the mystery of Christ there is no such thing as an individual, only a person in relationship, in baptismal and eucharistic communion, with God and other persons.**

LEARNING FROM THE MONASTICS

That is why in monasteries novices live in close contact with their spirit-filled elders and confess their thoughts to them at the end of each day, as we see in the book, *The Ladder of Divine Ascent*. To receive the gift of self-knowledge, one needs to open up to at least one other person, preferably a spiritual elder. To get to know our spiritual progress (or stagnation) we need to see ourselves reflected in the mirror of another person.

**The Journey into God.* Kenneth L. Bakken. Augsburg Publ., Mpls, MN. 2000.

Chapter Five

God has given us more than one such mirror: The mirror of God's word in Holy Scripture, the mirror of our loved ones at home, the mirror of a spiritual elder, even the mirror of our enemies as they reflect back to us some unpleasant things that just may be true about us.

Abba Dorotheos emphasized the danger of ignoring these mirrors when he wrote,

> *I know of no other fall for a monk except when he entrusts himself to his own heart. Some say that a person falls on account of this or that; but for my part, as I have already said, I know of no other fall except when a person goes his own way or follows his own will. Have you seen a fallen person? Know that he followed his own will. There is nothing more perilous, nothing more ruinous than this.*

DISCOVERING OUR REAL SELF THROUGH ONE'S SPOUSE

Marriage also is a great school for self-knowledge. In my premarital encounters with couples, I would say to them: We do not really know ourselves until we are married. We live too close to ourselves. It takes someone else to see us as we really are. This process of self-knowledge takes place especially in marriage—the most intimate of all relationships. The husband, for example, serves as a mirror. He reflects back to the wife her true personality as he sees it from the outside (and vice versa). The wife may not like what the husband sees and reflects back to her. And this is where we get much conflict in marriage. But if the wife would realize that neither of them is perfect, that marriage is an opportunity for them to get to know themselves better, I'm sure she would thank God for giving her a husband to show her what her weaknesses are so that she may correct them. We may prefer that God speak to us more directly than through our husbands or wives. But we may learn a great deal by listening to what He says to us through them. Let it be said that all of this must be done in utter humility and love.

Continuing the pre-marital encounter, we would then talk about what true love is as we encounter our spouse in marriage. Love is not "fulfilling" oneself through the use of another person. Love is giving oneself to another, for the good of the other, and receiving the other, and what he/she offers in the relationship, as a gift from God. This is the selfless path to self-knowledge.

DISCOVERING ONE'S REAL SELF THROUGH A SPIRITUAL ELDER

One of the great sources of self-knowledge in addition to relationships such as marriage is the spiritual elder whom Fr. John Chryssavgis describes as follows:

> *In the spiritual elder, the Church offers us someone with whom we can share our heart. This person is a benevolent companion who accompanies us on our spiritual journey. The spiritual father or mother is a fellow-traveler, not a tour guide. The bond that forms can be very intense, the relationship very intimate. This is made possible, in part, by the spiritual mentor's own purified condition and intense, intimate connection with the Holy Trinity. Though perhaps not yet fully glorified by God, ideally he or she possesses a purified heart in which the passions have been set aright and illumination*

has begun. *With such a person we will be able to surrender safely and most easily to the process of spiritual direction.**

"HUMAN BEINGS ARE GOD'S LANGUAGE"

We grow into self-knowledge as we live in relationship with God and other people. Relationships are central to our lives. Our learning, our work, the discovery of ourselves—all depend on relationships. We cannot truly know ourselves if we do not have other people to whom we can relate. It is only as I "face" another person, look into his eyes, relate to him, that I myself become a person and come to understand who I am. No one can become a person alone. Here we see the wisdom of the Hasidic saying, "Human beings are God's language." God uses human beings to speak to us, but it takes humility to listen, learn and grow.

For example, if someone says you have a problem with drinking too much, you can take it as an insult and lose your temper, or you can calm down and consider prayerfully that it just might be true and seek help before it destroys you. Or, if your spouse says you should spend more time at home, you can get angry, or you can listen and improve your family relationship before it is too late. God speaks to us through friends as well as enemies, but it takes humility to listen.

Barbara Brown Taylor relates the following interesting encounter she had:

> *Everyone needs someone to tell her she has spinach in her teeth, preferably before she has spent 15 minutes wondering why her table companions are so taken with*

* *Soul Mending: The Art of Spiritual Direction.* John Chryssavgis. HCO Press, Brookline, MA. 2000.

her smile. One friend recently crossed a gender boundary to help me with a similar problem lower down. "XYZ", he said, when we rose from eating lunch together.
"Huh?", I said.

"Examine your zipper," he said, and he was right. The fly on my Eddie Bauer summer sale jeans was standing wide open. As embarrassed as I was, I was grateful to him for being direct with me. He not only saved me from exposing myself all the way back to my car but also from spending the rest of the afternoon wondering if he had noticed.

We all need help seeing what we do not see, which is one reason we practice faith in community.*

Human beings are indeed God's language.

IMAGINARY SELVES

Pascal talked about the imaginary selves behind which we hide the real self. He wrote,

> We are not satisfied with the life we have in ourselves and our own being. We want to lead an imaginary life in the eyes of others, and so we try to make an impression. We strive constantly to embellish and preserve our imaginary being and neglect the real one.

We hide the real person (*prosopon*) behind the *prosopeion* (the mask). In fact, we do this so often as we keep disguising ourselves to others that we end up disguising ourselves to ourselves. We live an inauthentic life, the life of a lie. Sin, for

* *Christian Century.* August 24, 2004.

example, is not merely the transgression of an impersonal law; it is as Dr. Yannaras says, "missing the mark, failure to become one's self."

Fr. Harry Pappas once addressed this point in the following words that apply painfully to each one of us: "A powerful dynamic in human life is self-delusion: lack of authentic awareness of our own sinfulness, combined with an all-too-ready noticing of the sins of others. We are all quite guilty of hypocritically observing the speck in someone else's eye and missing the much greater log in our own eye (Matthew 7:3)."

This is what makes knowing, discovering one's true self, so difficult.

FAWNING BEFORE THE OPINION OF OTHERS

Fr. Alexander Elchaninov describes how we fawn before the opinion of others, allowing the opinion of others to smother the real self:

> *The opinion of others concerning us—that is the mirror before which we all, almost without exception, pose. A man tries to be such as he wishes to appear to others. The real man, as he actually is, remains unknown to all, often himself included, while a figure projected and embellished by the imagination conducts his life. This tendency to deceive is so great that, distorting his very nature, a man will sacrifice his own self, the unique and inimitable essence of his human personality.**

---

* *The Diary of a Russian Priest.* Alexander Elchaninov. SVS Press, Crestwood, NY. 1982.

We must add that fawning before the opinion of others and trying to be someone you're not is one of the hardest things in the world. Pretending can become tiring, frustrating, painful. Wearing a mask to hide the real person gets horribly uncomfortable and trying to cram ourselves into a mold that does not fit is highly procrustean and unnatural.

As Pascal said to Mitton, "The self is hateful. You cover it up, Mitton, but that does not mean that you take it away. So you are still hateful." Mitton was a worldly gambler and friend of Pascal.

THE NEED FOR A SPIRITUAL NAVIGATOR

Mitton was blessed to have a friend like Pascal to reflect back to him his hateful self. Self-knowledge is not possible without a spiritual mentor. In the words of St. Gregory Palamas:

> *If a man is unlikely to take an unexplored path without a true guide; if no one will risk going to sea without a skillful navigator; if no man will undertake to learn a science or an art without an experienced teacher, who will dare to attempt a practical study of the art of arts and the science of sciences, to enter the mysterious path leading to God, and venture to sail the boundless mental sea, that is monastic life, akin to the life of the angels, and be sure of reaching his goal without a guide, a navigator and a true and experienced teacher?*

The role of the spiritual navigator or guide is to help us hear what the Holy Spirit is saying and to see ourselves clearly in the eyes of another. This is critical because whatever is received by us is received according to the mode of the receiver. We see as we are. We hear as we are. We understand as we are. Perception can be distorted by jealousy, envy, pride and a whole array of negative passions and emotions. All these can undermine us and keep us from understanding the truth and discovering our true selves. The role of the spiritual guide in self-knowledge is critical.

One of the greatest spiritual mentors of the 19th century was Dostoevsky about whom his biographer wrote:

> *Dostoevsky's psychological art is famous throughout the world. Long before Freud and before the school of psychoanalysts he plunged into the depths of the subconscious and investigated the inner life of children and adolescents; he studied the psychics of insane, maniacs, fanatics, criminals, suicides. Special commentaries exist on Dostoevsky, the psychopathologist and criminalist. But his analysis was not limited to individual psychology; he penetrated the collective psychology of the family, of society, of the people.**

What really animated Dostoevsky, writes his biographer, was "the radiant image of the Christ, love for whom was the greatest love of his whole life." Such insight into human lives was truly a gift of the Holy Spirit. It came through great suffering and pain. "My hosanna has passed through a great furnace of doubt," he wrote.

A DOUBLE MIRROR

Thus, when through the double mirror of Christ and our loved ones, we come to see ourselves as we truly are, are ashamed of ourselves, have difficulty accepting ourselves, we can be sure of one thing—Christ *will* accept us. We are not saying that Christ

---

* *Dostoevsky: His Life and Work.* Konstantine Mochlusky. Translated by Michael A. Miniham. Princeton Univ. Press. 1967.

is satisfied with us the way we are, or that He will be content to have us remain forever as imperfect as we are now. What we are saying is that when we repent and cling to Him in faith, Jesus will accept us, grant us new life and a profound insight into our true self.

About nothing else is Jesus more emphatic. "Him that cometh to me I will in no way cast out." He can deliver us from self-pity and self-excuse. He can help remove the many layers of self-deceit from our hearts to help us discover the image of God in us and lead us to union with Him (Theosis).

To "know thyself" alone may mean that you sink into despair, but to "know thyself" and find your true self in Christ is to find acceptance, forgiveness and power to rise above sin and despair to a new self, your true self, your best self.

– Chapter Six –

Chapter Six

FINDING ONE'S TRUE SELF IN GOD
(Part One)

We are who we are by virtue of God's having created us in His own Trinitarian likeness.... This is our true identity, "true" in the sense of "best".
—Ellen Charry

There is only one true, realistic, and honest way for man to be aware of himself. It is to be first aware of God. For it is God who has created man's soul in his own likeness. When man then becomes aware of himself, he finds himself at once facing God's likeness.
—Matthew the Poor

It was you Who created my inmost self and put me together in my mother's womb. You know me through and through, from having watched my bones take shape when I was being formed in secret (Ps. 139:13-15). Before I formed you in the womb, I knew you (Jer. 1:5).

FIND YOUR TRUE SELF IN GOD

We find our true self not by running from psychologist to psychiatrist, anxiously trying to affirm ourselves or be affirmed, while at the same time remaining blind to the One Who loved us first, Who seeks to dwell in our heart and has formed our true self in His own image. It is sad that many are content to stay on the psychiatrist's couch in their search for their true self, even though such psychoanalysis rarely helps one experience the true "I" which is discovered only in God.

Origen maintained that our first task is to find our true self in the image and likeness of God in which we were created. Man finds his authentic self in the Archetype or image of the One in whose likeness he was created: Jesus. That is why Pascal said that "We know nothing of ourselves but by Jesus alone." If we are made in the divine image, then we can know ourselves only as we come to know and conform to the image in which we were made. We come to realize that not only our being but our very destiny is God-like. Dostoevsky wrote that "the nature of man is correlative to the nature of God; if there is no God, there is also no man. We got rid of the God-man and we established a man-god."

Ours is the exalted destiny of knowing that we are made by God and for God; we are made for participating in the very nature of God through theosis. This is why St. Basil speaks of human identity in terms of "the dignity of bearing God's image". Thus, we are called to live out our God-created identity, to grow by God's grace from the image of God in which we were created to the likeness of God in Christ. That is where we will find our true self.

— Chapter Six —

SELF-ACTUALIZATION IN CHRIST

Ellen Charry explains the implications of this when she writes, "The self-actualization and self-realization language of the mid-twentieth century psychology is Christian psychology divorced from its foundation and grafted onto the root of the secular self. Returned to its proper Christian context, salvation is self-realization, that is, realization of our true identity in God—growing into it and using it fruitfully."* She adds, "If God is triune, and we are made in the divine image, then we understand ourselves properly only through the triune identity itself…. Our very being is God-like."**

To know my spiritual identity, to know who I truly am, I must come to know Jesus, the One in whose image I was made.

I like what Fr. Christopher Metropoulos once wrote in this respect,

> *If my relationship with God is weak or even non-existent, then it follows that I will never authentically know myself. And being ignorant of myself, I will forever be missing the mark of my true calling and my true meaning.*

"YOU ARE MADE COMPLETE IN HIM"

Being truly human says St. Paul, means becoming Christified. "In Christ all the fullness of the Godhead dwells bodily. And you are complete in Him…"(Col. 2:9-10). "We are transformed into the same image (of Christ) from glory to glory" (2 Cor. 3:18). The Gospels offer us a beautiful description of the Person of Jesus in whose image we are made

---

* *Theology Today*. October 2004.
** Ibid.

and into whose image we are being transformed from glory to glory. It is in Him that we find our true self, our best self. It is in Him that we are made "complete". We achieve "self-actualization" and "self-realization" in the God-Man, Jesus the Christ, who said, "I am the Way...." He is our way to know God and to know ourselves in the light of our true destiny as revealed in his Word. A relationship with God is our true identity. After all, He is our Father and we are His Children.

SEEKING TO FIND OURSELVES IN THE ARCHETYPE

George MacDonald, the writer who inspired C.S. Lewis, wrote something worth pondering concerning finding one's true self in God:

"I hope you don't think God made us, and made the world, out of nothing. I don't believe God made anything out of nothing; I think He made all things out of Himself. And making us thus out of Himself, the problem was how to make us so that we should be ourselves; and so I sometimes think He took a great trouble *to throw us off, as it were, so far out of Himself as that we might become ourselves*, and develop a will and a free will of our own, and with that free will turn around and seek Him."

Having created us in His image and given us free will, God expects us to use our free will to seek Him who is our archetype, the original blueprint of our humanity, but He wants us to do so freely. Christ is what God had in mind as a model for us when he created us. In the words of St. Nicholas Cabasilas, "It was toward Christ that man's mind and desire were oriented. We were given a mind that we might know

– Chapter Six –

Christ, and desire that we might run to Him, and memory that we might remember Him, because even at the time of creation, it was He who was the archetype."

The gospel calls on us continually to make Christ the center and purpose of our lives as did St. Paul, "I live yet not I but Christ lives in me." In Christ our homesick soul will find not only its true self but also its true love. In the safety of that home, the sadnesses of life will drive us into the loving embrace of the One whose love for us is beyond comprehension.

Thus, only in God becoming Man do we gain the possibility of true personhood. In the words of St. Nicholas Cabasilas, "The birth of Christ is the true birthday of mankind."

St. Gregory Palamas sums it up, "The original creation of man formed in the image of God, was for the sake of Christ, so that Man should be able one day to make room for the Archetype."

WE ARE HIS "HOMIEST HOME"

The Bible says that God is omnipresent. He dwells everywhere. Everywhere is His. Yet in all of creation there is no place He likes to call home more than the human heart. Of all that He has made, we are His favorite dwelling place. He craves to find a home of love within us. As Dame Julian of Norwich, that delightful English mystic said, "We are God's dream, His homiest home." "If anyone loves me," said Jesus, "he will keep My word; and My Father will love him, and We will come to him and make Our home with him" (John 14:23). Julian of Norwich once described how Jesus comes to "make His home" in us:

> Mothers give their children milk to suck, but Jesus is the sweet Mother who feeds us with Himself. His kindness accomplishes this when we eat the holy Eucharist. This priceless food is life itself, and that's why it strengthens us and helps us grow....
>
> Mothers also lay their children down on their breasts, for rest and succor, but Jesus is the gentlest Mother who takes us by the hand and leads us into God's breast through His own satisfying open side. I saw Jesus look down there at His gashed side and smile and say to me, "Look here and see how I love you."

He already loves us. We are self-realized and self-actualized only as we, in turn, love Him with all our mind, heart, soul and strength.

> For great is the dignity of humanity. See how great are the heavens and the earth, the sun and the moon. But the Lord was not pleased to find his rest in them but in humanity alone. Man, therefore, is of greater value than all other creatures, and perhaps, I will not hesitate to say, not only visible creatures, but also those invisible, namely, "the ministering spirits" (Heb. 1:14). For it was not of Michael or Gabriel the archangels, that God said: "Let us make man according to our image and likeness" (Gn. 1:26), but he said it concerning the spiritual makeup of the human, I mean, the immortal soul.
> —St. Macarius

MAN FULLY ALIVE IS THE GLORY OF GOD

Self-knowledge is impossible without God. Jean-Paul Sartre and other twentieth century atheist philosophers have shown how empty and pointless life is without God. Man cannot be understood in a purely closed system, i.e., in a humanistic framework without God. Why? Because man is constantly looking for something beyond himself, something that his nature cannot supply. Dissatisfied with this world he yearns for transcendence. "O Lord, our hearts are restless until they find their rest in Thee," prayed Augustine.

Irenaeus wrote, "The glory of God is man fully alive." He means fully alive to God. For then it is that man becomes authentically human when he is fully alive to God. Such a man is not only "God's glory"; Irenaeus adds, "Such a man is "the vision of the glory of God". In other words, life makes sense and finds meaning only when it is focused on "the vision of God" in Christ. When that happens, God is glorified and manifests Himself in the world primarily through man, the crown of His creation. Self-actualized man finds his purpose in life in knowing, loving and serving God. "The glory of God is man fully alive, and the life of man is the vision of the glory of God" (St. Irenaeus).

AN ANIMAL IN PROCESS OF DEIFICATION

St. Gregory of Nazianzus defines the human being as "an animal in the process of being deified"—in Greek *zoon theoumenon*. This is what sets us apart from the rest of creation, i.e., our calling to become "partakers of divine nature", gods by grace, partakers of God's glory. This is what defines an authentically human life. Created in the image of the Triune God, we find our true selves in the image of the Triune God.

A DIRECT BREATHING IN OF DIVINE LIFE

In Genesis 2:7 we read that man was shaped from dust as were the animals, but unlike the animals, man was given a direct "breathing in" of divine life. God "breathed into his nostrils the breath of life; and man became a living soul" (Gen. 2:7). This divine breath, together with the divine image (Gen. 1:27) sets man apart from the animals.

This is what makes man the glory of God. Once God is removed from the equation, however, man degenerates into "a mere quintessence of dust". With God man becomes a *microtheos* (a little god) according to Gregory of Nyssa and Maximus the Confessor. C.S. Lewis alluded to this when he wrote that every person we encounter has "the potential to be something, which if we saw it in all its truth and glory, we would be tempted to bow down to and worship."*

OUR IDENTITY IS "HIDDEN WITH CHRIST IN GOD"

This great mystery is a gift of God's grace. It begins to happen in baptism about which St. Paul writes, "Because you have died, the life you now have is hidden with Christ in God ... Christ is your life ... you too will be revealed in all your glory with Christ" (Col. 3:1-4). When Paul uses the word "life" here, he is referring to the fact that God is our very being. As he said to the Athenians "For in Him, we live and move and have our being" (Acts 17: 28). He is speaking of our deepest being, our true self as something that is "hidden with Christ in God". This is the foundational core of what we call our identity, which is

---

* *The Weight of Glory.* C.S. Lewis (New York: Macmillan 1980).

– Chapter Six –

mystically utterly caught up in God, "in whom we live and move and have our being", and in whom our very self is immersed.

What begins in baptism is completed in the other two sacraments of Chrismation and the Eucharist through which the true self is united with the Trinity. Thus, the three sacraments of initiation become the sacraments of our deepest identity, hidden in the self-emptying of God in Christ.

FROM BIOS LIFE TO ZOE LIFE

The potential in us comes about, wrote C.S. Lewis, when the *Bios* life, the biological life that we share with the animals, is changed by God's grace to the *Zoe* life, which is the spiritual life, the life in the Triune God from all eternity. "A man who changed from having *Bios* life to having *Zoe* life," says Lewis, "would have gone through as big a change as a statue which changed from being a carved stone to being a real man."

That is exactly the change that takes place when we find our true self in Christ and are Christified. The very blood of the Son of God flows in our veins, imparting to us divine life, transforming statues into living images of God.

Matthew the Poor wrote,

> *There is only one true, realistic and honest way for man to be aware of himself. It is to be first aware of God. For it is God who has created man's soul in his own likeness. When man then becomes aware of himself, he finds himself at once facing God's likeness.**

---

* *Orthodox Prayer Life: The Interior Way.* Matthew the Poor. SVS Publishing, Scarsdale, NY. 2003.

St. John Chrysostom adds,

> Find the door of the inner chamber of your soul and you will discover that this is the door into the kingdom of Heaven.... Therefore, to find God we must dig in search of this inner chamber...where God and we can meet.

St. Isaac the Syrian's words echo the same truth:

> The ladder that leads to the kingdom is hidden in your soul. Flee from sin, dive into yourself, and in your soul you will discover the stairs by which to ascend.

TODAY'S JOURNEY INTO THE "INNER CHAMBER" DISCOVERS NOT GOD BUT A SEWER

It is unfortunate that today man's journey to the "inner chamber" to discover God and one's true self has been totally distorted. Self-knowledge has now degenerated to the point where when a person discovers that he or she is gay, the gayness is considered as a discovery of the true self and the real person "comes out". Orthodox Christians do not identify themselves by their sin. "I am an alcoholic." "I am an homosexual." "I am a lesbian."

Dr. Steven Robinson wrote,

> The Christian faith teaches us that we are all created in the image of God. The Fathers teach that the image may be marred, corroded, covered, but it is never lost. While those in the world may lay claim to their sin as a label or a badge, those who are Christians are not labeled with

— Chapter Six —

> *their sin, but are merely Christ-ians: in the image of Christ. We either bear the name of Christ, or we bear the name of our sins. St. Paul says no "fornicators, idolaters, nor adulterers, nor effeminate, nor homosexuals, nor thieves, nor covetous, nor drunkards, nor revilers, nor swindlers, shall inherit the kingdom of God, and such were some of you but you were washed, but you were sanctified, but you were justified in the name of the Lord Jesus Christ and in the Spirit of God" (1 Cor. 6:9-11 NASV).*
>
> *When we enter the arena of the Church and the struggle against sin, we are no longer labeled with our sin. This is true of heterosexual sin, homosexual sin, or any other sin. We are not defined by the gender of the person for whom we have a sexual desire, but by Christ. The Church is only concerned with who you are becoming in Christ through the practice of the virtues, regardless of your besetting sin.**

Orthodox Christians do not believe that they are "totally depraved" because of original sin. Our sinful condition is not our true nature. We are defined by the image of God in us which is our true nature. Though the image is marred, it is not totally lost.

HOMOSEXUALITY: ONE OF THE PASSIONS

Fr. Stanley Harakas, professor emeritus of Ethics, describes homosexuality as one of the many passions we inherit from Adam against which we are called to struggle and overcome through prayer and ascesis. He writes:

---

* *AGAIN Magazine.* Spring. 2006. Vol. 28, No. 1. Published by Conciliar Press, Goleta, CA.

In the language of the Church, this (homosexuality) is a "passion". It is a wrongful orientation of our desires. Passions are of many kinds, directed toward many objects, such as self (pride), money (greed), food (gluttony), extramarital sex partners (lust), others' property (theft), etc. When such passions exist, no matter how strongly felt, the Church counsels agona, that is, spiritual and moral struggle against them. In our commonly shared struggle against sin in whatever form, the Orthodox Church sees all persons working to fight temptation and overcome the passions. Toward this end the Church offers a panoply of spiritual weapons to overcome temptation and to struggle victoriously against the passions. These spiritual weapons include prayer, worship, fasting, the Sacrament of Holy Confession, reading Scripture and spiritual writings, Christian fellowship, as well as pastoral and psychiatric counseling which should be used by all including those who suffer from homosexual tendencies.*

SAME SEX ATTRACTION

For those who wish to pursue further what the Orthodox Church teaches concerning same-sex attraction, we recommend a recent book by Fr. Thomas Hopko entitled *Orthodox Christian Faith and Same-Sex Attraction*, published by Conciliar press, Goleta, CA in 2006.

I share with you the following paragraph from Fr. Hopko's excellent book:

> The tragic truth, however, is that countless people, especially in contemporary secularized societies, have

---
* *Contemporary Moral Issues.* Stanley Harakas. Light and Life Publ. Co., Mpls, MN. 1982.

become convinced that their sinful thoughts and feelings, including, and even especially, those having to do with sex, are perfectly normal and natural and, as such, define who they are in their essential being and life. They therefore see no purpose or need in resisting, disciplining, and ultimately destroying them. They are convinced, on the contrary, that to do so would be dishonest, would be to deny and destroy themselves as persons, and, as such, would result in their personal death, which, according to Christian Orthodoxy, is the exact opposite of the truth.

IS THERE HOPE?

Is there hope for those who are enslaved by the passions of the flesh? There most certainly is! Having fought the passions personally the Fathers of the Church have charted a way of victory for us. Echoing the words of the Apostle Paul, "And those who belong to Christ Jesus have crucified the flesh with its passions and desires" (Gal. 5:24), they demonstrate exactly how "the passions and desires" of the flesh can be crucified.

ST. MACARIUS ON THE UNFATHOMABLE DEPTHS OF THE HEART

It is not strange that the practitioners of the American Religion (Gnosticism) find not God but a veritable sewer when they delve into themselves. St. Macarius wrote about this centuries ago in his *Homilies*:

Within the heart are unfathomable depths. There are reception rooms and bedchambers in it, doors and porches, and many offices and passages. In it is the workshop of righteousness and of wickedness. In it is death; in it is life.... The heart is but a small vessel: and yet dragons and lions are there, and there poisonous creatures and all the treasures of wickedness; rough, uneven paths are there, and gaping chasms. There likewise is God, there are angels, there life and the Kingdom, there light and the apostles, the heavenly cities and the treasures of grace: all things are there.

The pure in heart will find God when they descend into the inner chamber; the impure in heart will discover in that inner chamber not God but "dragons and lions and poisonous creatures and all the treasures of wickedness, rough uneven paths and gaping chasms."

It is unfortunate that even religion is being used to rationalize and declare as normal that which is abnormal,to cover up the real self (the image of God) with a false self, consisting of one or more of the passions.

HATE THE SIN; LOVE THE SINNER

We emphasize that no Christian should ever point a finger at another person. We are all sinners in need of redemption. Same-sex attraction, when acted upon, is a sin but so is greed, lust, gluttony and a host of other sins. What we must not do, however, is sit back and allow the secular world to convince us through bogus research that same-sex attraction is not only normal but also a "civil right". If it is a civil right, then kleptomania, polygamy and pedophilia also need to be proclaimed "civil rights". We live in a broken world where some people's sexuality is broken. These people need all the love we can give them, all the prayer, all the compassion, all the

– Chapter Six –

understanding. Hate the sin; love the sinner. What these people do not need is to be affirmed as "normal". We are all sick, living in a fallen world. Healing comes not when we deny our sickness but when we acknowledge it and bring it to God for healing. "Bear one another's burdens and so fulfill the law of Christ" (Gal. 6:2).

Chapter Seven

FINDING ONE'S TRUE SELF IN GOD
(Part Two)

Why do you fail to see in yourself the same fault you censure in others? If you put up with yourself, why not put up with everyone else? Rather than be a presumptuous controller of others, be a good companion. Flee from your own faults. The faults of others will not hurt you. Never rejoice if you are better than others. Be sorry that they are not better and accept responsibility for it. If you need to hate someone, hate yourself. No one else has hurt you more.*

The standard for understanding and judging man is not man himself but the God-Man.
—Constantine B. Scouteris

"The ontological truth of man does not lie in himself conceived as an autonomous being...No. It lies in the archetype. Since man is an image, his real being is not defined by the created element with which he is constructed...but by his uncreated Archetype...and his Archetype is Christ."
—Panayiotis Nellas

---

* Guigo 1: *Meditations*.

— Chapter Seven —

WHERE CAN WE FIND OUR TRUE SELF?

When Socrates wrote, "Know Thyself", he could have made it easier for us. He could have told us in whom we could find our true self if he had added, "Know thyself *and God*". For it is in God that we can come to know our true self. It is in His image that we are made. He is the prototype. We are His living images. Clement of Alexandria prioritized self-knowledge as the greatest of all sciences when he wrote, "It is the greatest of all sciences to know one's self. For whoever knows one's self will know God; and in knowing God, will become like God." That is why the corollary to truly knowing one's self in Christ is theosis, sharing in God's nature. God made us free so that finding our true image in Him, we would freely proceed to grow in Christ-likeness.

"IF I KNEW MYSELF I SHOULD KNOW THEE"

God can be known through His image in each one of us. St. Cyprian of Carthage said, "That you may acquaint yourself with God, first become acquainted with yourself." Isaac the Syrian explained how we can find God in the self when he wrote, "Strive to enter the treasury within you and you will see the heavenly treasury; for the two are one and the same. By entering one, you will see both. The ladder to that kingdom is within you, hidden in your soul." Elsewhere St. Isaac writes, "If you are pure, heaven is within you; within yourself you will see the angels and the Lord of angels." St. Maximus the Confessor wrote that "God is hidden in the hearts of those who believe in Him. They shall see Him when they have purified themselves through love and self-control; and the greater the purity, the more they shall see." St. Gregory of Nyssa explained, "If a man's heart has been purified from every creature and all unruly affections, he will see the image of the Divine Nature in his own beauty." Thus, it is that knowledge of self leads to knowledge of God. "If I knew myself, I should know Thee, " prayed Augustine.

KNOWING ONESELF THROUGH PURITY OF HEART

Purity of heart enables us to know not only God but ourselves and others, as we and they truly are. "Create in me a clean heart, O God, and put a new and right spirit within me" (Psalm 51:10).

If purity of heart is necessary to see God, it is just as necessary to help us discover ourselves as reflected in God's image. This is perhaps why C.S. Lewis wrote,

> *While in other sciences the instruments you use are things external to yourself (things like microscopes and telescopes), the instrument through which you see God is your whole self. And if a man's self isn't kept clean and bright, his glimpse of God will be blurred—like the Moon seen through a dirty telescope. That's why horrible nations have horrible religions: they've been looking at God through a dirty lens.*

St. Nektarios of Aegina adds,

> *The Divine light illuminates the pure heart and the pure intellect, because these are susceptible of receiving light; whereas impure hearts and intellects, not being susceptible of receiving illumination, have an aversion for*

Chapter Seven

> the light of knowledge, the light of truth—they like darkness.

No crime looks so bad to the man who has committed it as to the man who has kept clear of it. As soon as we have done something that is nasty, we have blunted our own capacity to be disgusted; we have tarnished the mirror in which we are to look at our own reflection. The mirror of the soul must be kept clean. "Blessed are the pure in heart, for they shall see God." "The greater the purity, the more they shall see" (Maximos the Confessor).

THE HIPPIE AND GOD

A hippie walked into a psychiatrist's office one day, smoking pot and wearing love beads, frayed bellbottom trousers and shoulder-length hair.

The psychiatrist said, "You claim you are not a hippie. Then how do you explain the clothes, the hair, the pot?"

"That's what I'm here to find out, Doc," said the hippie.

The truth is that he was not a hippie. He had made himself a hippie, whereas God had made him in His own image, a living icon of God. He needed more than a psychiatrist to help him find his true self. He needed God, the Church, the Bible, and a spiritual mother or father.

When a pagan asked Theophilus of Antioch, "Show me thy God," he replied, "Show me yourself, and I will show you my God." He meant your true self—the image of God in you.

Bede Griffith, a Western monastic, expressed it this way,

> *To discover God*
> *is not to discover an idea*
> *but to discover oneself.*
> *It is to awaken*
> *to that part of one's existence*
> *which has been hidden from sight*
> *and which one has refused to recognize.*
>
> *The discovery may be very painful;*
> *it is like going through*
> *a kind of death.*
>
> *But it is the one thing*
> *which makes life*
> *worth living.*

WE ARE GOD-SOURCED AND GOD-SHAPED

Not only does knowing one's self make life worth living, it is in fact the very purpose of life.

Philip Sherrard explained the process of knowing one's self in God in a masterful way when he wrote,

> *I shall not understand who I am, and so I shall not understand what the world is, unless I realize that I am formed in the image of God—a created expression of God's infinite self-expression. If I work not from above downwards but from below upwards, as the theory of evolution does—if I see myself simply as a kind of superior ape, in whom self-consciousness has emerged as*

— Chapter Seven —

> an epiphenomenon of some physical process—then I shall fatally misinterpret my own self, and so I shall have a distorted view of everything else as well. "Know yourself" means "Know yourself as God-sourced, God-shaped", acknowledge your divine origin, recognize that you are a sacred being. Apart from God we are unintelligible as human persons. The divine is the determining element in our humanness; losing our sense of the divine we lose also our sense of the human. God is the inmost center of our reality.... The very concept of man implies a relationship, a connection with God. Where one affirms man one also affirms God.*

"Made in God's image," writes Bishop Ware, "man is the mirror of the divine. He knows God by knowing himself: entering within himself, he sees God reflected in the purity of his own heart."**

Julian of Norwich expressed it this way, "Our soul is kindly rooted in God in endless love. And therefore, if we want to have knowing of our soul and communion and loving with it, we need to seek into our God, in whom it is enclosed."

> God is your being, and what you are, you are in God ....
> But you are not God's being....
> —The author of The Cloud

THE UGLY DUCKLING

The story of the Ugly Duckling may help us at this point. The poor creature was too large compared to the ducks, his neck was too long, and he was, to put it mildly, awkward and clumsy—a swan in the midst of ducks. He became the object of ridicule in

* *The Rape of Man and Nature.* Philip Sherrard.
** *The Orthodox Way.* Kallistos Ware. SVS Press, Crestwood, NY. 1979.

the duck community. Then one day—miracle of miracles—he had a special revelation. He discovered that the reason he was such a failure was that he was not a duck at all. He was a swan. Once he learned his true identity, his whole life changed. The other swans in the castle moat greeted him and surrounded him with love and respect. Everything changed when he discovered who he really was and where he belonged.

The story of the Ugly Duckling is really our story. We were created in the image of God, which means that we were created to live in fellowship, in communion with God and to be part of God's family. But throughout history people have failed to act as God's children. They acted as if they neither belonged to God nor needed God. So it is that when we discover the image of God in us and return to Him, we discover who we really are and are welcomed home by the waiting Father.

WE FIND THE TRUTH ABOUT OURSELVES IN CHRIST

It is in meeting God in Christ that we find the truth about ourselves. Meeting God disintegrates the illusions we have about ourselves and exposes the masks we wear. Pascal expressed this well when he wrote, "Jesus Christ is the object of all things, the center towards which all things tend. Whoever knows Him knows the reason for everything." Jesus removes the scales from our eyes, enabling us to discover our true identity in Him as "God-shaped and God-sourced" (Philip Sherrard).

Pavel Florensky emphasizes that God has revealed our true self (image) to us in His Son:

– Chapter Seven –

> *It is the image of God, purified of original sin. In Himself, the Lord showed every man precisely himself as he is, in his incorruptible original beauty. As in a clean mirror, the Lord allowed every man to see the holiness of his own undesecrated image of God. In "Man" or the "Son of Man", the fullness of his own personality is revealed to every man. This provides the "apperceiving mass" for inner seekings; this point of light marks the direction for a wandering conscience.**

Being able to look inside ourselves with God is a crucial part of knowing ourselves, of setting ourselves free from the passions that prevent us from knowing ourselves. Abba Poemen said, "Not understanding what has happened (to us) prevents us from going on to something better." Knowing oneself is basic to repentance and redemption.

> *When the mind has divested itself of its fallen state and has clothed itself with the state of grace, then in the time of prayer it can even see its own inner condition, which is something like a sapphire or the azure blue of the sky. Scripture calls this the dwelling place of God, which the elders saw on Mount Sinai.*
> —Evagrios of Pontus

GOD EXPOSES IN ORDER TO HEAL

We may choose to wear masks to conceal our real self, but God wants to heal us, and to do that, He must first expose the masks we wear. As One who exposes, God is in the business of making the unknown known by exposing the lies manufactured by our ego-defence system. He exposes our secrets because concealed sin is a cancer that eats away at the spiritual life (*Zoe*) within

---
* *The Pillar and Ground of Truth.* Pavel Florensky. Princeton Univ. Press, Princeton, NJ.

us. The doorway to discovering our real self and proceeding to renewal and newness of life is admitting the truth about ourselves. And this can happen only when we come to Christ, the Light of the World, the Divine Illuminator, Who dissolves all pretense and reveals the truth to us; truth that liberates from passions and lies, and becomes our call to freedom. Thus, the shortest way to self-knowledge is to draw near to the Light of the World.

C.S. Lewis once said, "When a man is getting better, he understands more and more clearly the evil that is still in him. When a man is getting worse, he understands his own badness less and less. A moderately bad man knows he is not very good; a thoroughly bad man thinks he is all right…. Good people know about both good and evil; bad people do not know about either." "Those in the grip of an illusion never recognize their affliction," said Freud. "A beast does not know that he is a beast, and the nearer a man gets to being a beast, the less he knows it," said George Macdonald.

That is why the Church Fathers counsel us to struggle against our passions. The more we struggle against them, the better we know ourselves. The more we yield to them, the less we understand ourselves. So, says C.S. Lewis, "Virtue—even attempted virtue—brings light; indulgence brings fog."

Passions lead to what the Church Fathers call *plani*, spiritual delusion. Fr. Maximos of Mount Athos calls *plani* (delusion) the worst evil that can befall a person. He says,

> *We often meet highly educated people who are so proud of their own achievements that they are completely uninterested in and incapable of hearing what the other*

— Chapter Seven —

*person has to say. They know it all. This is a serious spiritual affliction, a really demonic symptom, believe me. The devil does not accept any advice. He does not give up his own opinions and perceptions. He never doubts himself.**

ST. SILOUAN

St. Silouan the Athonite wrote, "It is only...after much wrestling against the passions, much reading of the Scriptures and the works of the holy Fathers, and many discussions with spiritual guides and other ascetics, that man discovers in himself the light of the knowledge of the ways of the spirit, which comes secretly and unobserved."

The passions need to be eradicated because they delude us, blinding us to our real self. The Holy Scriptures need to be studied because it is in them that we truly discover who we are. In the words of Fulgence of Ruspe (468-533),

> *Study your heart in the light of the Holy Scriptures, and you will know therein who you were, who you are, and who you ought to be.*

KNOWING ONESELF THROUGH THE JESUS PRAYER

The Jesus Prayer is an effective way of helping us attain self-knowledge. Praying the Jesus Prayer regularly helps us develop the opportunity to observe what is going on inside ourselves; it helps us discriminate between the good and the bad thoughts that seek entrance. Praying the Jesus Prayer encourages and

---

* *Gifts of the Desert.* Kyriacos C. Markides. Doubleday, A Division of Random House, New York, NY 2005.

strengthens the good, and helps us reject the bad. Through this process we are enabled over a period of time to know ourselves in a deep and profound way.

This was the experience of the anonymous Russian pilgrim who testifies in *The Way of a Pilgrim*:

> *Silently descend into the depths of your heart. Call on the name of Jesus Christ frequently. This is the way to experience interior illumination. Many things will become clear to you, even the mysteries of the kingdom of God. You will discover a depth of mystery, a brightness, when you learn to descend into yourself! The truth is: we are aliens to ourselves. We have little desire to know ourselves. We run after many things in this world, and by doing so run away from ourselves. We exchange truth for trinkets.*

"To know yourself means that you must guard yourself diligently from everything external to you," wrote Nikitas Stithatos. The *Philokalia* teaches that knowing oneself is attained by posting a guard at the entrance to one's mind and prayerfully controlling the thoughts that enter. How? Through *prosoche* (vigilance) and *proseuche* (prayer). In the words of St. Gregory Palamas:

> *"Be attentive to yourself," says Moses (Deut 15:9. LXX)—that is, to the whole of yourself, not to a few things that pertain to you, neglecting the rest. By what means? With the intellect assuredly, for nothing else can pay attention to the whole of yourself. Set this guard, therefore, over your soul and body, for thereby you will readily free yourself from the evil passions of body and*

> soul. Take yourself in hand, then, be attentive to yourself, scrutinize yourself; or, rather guard, watch over and test yourself, for in this manner you will subdue your rebellious unregenerate self to the spirit and there will never again be "some secret iniquity in your heart" (Deut 15:9).

GIVING OURSELVES TO CHRIST

In addition to vigilance of mind, another way to self-knowledge is by surrendering ourselves to Christ: "Let us commit ourselves and one another and our whole life to Christ our Lord," we pray in the liturgy. There must be a real giving of oneself to Christ. C.S. Lewis expressed it strongly when he wrote,

> *Give up your self, and you will find your real self. Lose your life, and you will save it. Submit to death, death of your ambitions and favourite wishes every day and death of your whole body in the end: submit with every fibre of your being, and you will find eternal life. Keep back nothing. Nothing that you have not given away will ever be really yours. Nothing in you that has not died will ever be raised from the dead. Look for yourself, and you will find in the long run only hatred, loneliness, despair, rage, ruin, and decay. But look for Christ and you will find Him, and with Him everything else thrown in....*
>
> *Most of what I call "Me" can be very easily explained. It is when I turn to Christ, when I give myself up to His Personality, that I first begin to have a real personality of my own.... There are no real personalities anywhere else. Until you have given up your self to Him, you will not*

have a real self. *Sameness is to be found most among the most "natural" men, not among those who surrender to Christ. How monotonously alike all the great tyrants and conquerors have been: how gloriously different are the saints.*

True self-knowledge comes from giving one's life to Jesus as Lord, "losing one's life in order to find it", as Jesus said.

Such profound insight into ourselves can come only from God.

SELF-FULFILLMENT VERSUS GOD-FULFILLMENT

We will not find ourselves in self-fulfillment; only in God-fulfillment. We live in a culture that has produced an entire industry in trying to teach us how to "find" ourselves. Christ came to tell us that we cannot find ourselves unless we lose ourselves in Him and for Him. It is when the self is subordinated to Christ that we come to a new understanding of who we are because we come to know whose we are.

> *Our real selves are all waiting for us in [God]. It is no good trying to "be myself" without him. The more I resist him and try to live on my own, the more I become dominated by my own heredity and upbringing and surroundings and natural desires.*
> —C.S. Lewis

ST. PAUL KNOWS HIMSELF AS THE CHIEF OF SINNERS

When asked once what was wrong with the world, G.K.

— Chapter Seven —

Chesterton replied, "I am." We are all guilty for the good we could have done, but did not do. The transformation of the world begins with my personal transformation and resurrection in Christ. Such was the self-knowledge St. Paul had of himself when he referred to himself as the chief of sinners, which is reflected in the pre-communion prayer we pray in each liturgy:

> *I believe, O Lord, and I confess that You are in truth the Christ, the Son of the living God, who came in the world to save the sinners of whom I am the first.*

Such self-knowledge is born of vigilance, prayer, humility and repentance. It is truly a gift of the Holy Spirit. "To see your sins in all their multiplicity and hideousness is indeed a gift of God," wrote St. John of Kronstad. A prime example of such divinely inspired self-knowledge is the following Pre-Communion Prayer written by St. Simeon, the New Theologian:

> *Behold, mine iniquities have exceeded the number of the hairs upon my head. For what evil is there that I have not done? What sin is there that I have not committed? What evil thing is there that I have not meditated in my soul? I am guilty of fornication and of adultery, of pride, arrogance, condemnation of others, censure, idle conversation, unworthy laughter, drunkenness, gluttony, hatred, envy, cupidity, avarice, usury, self-love, ambition, rapacity; of untruthfulness, unjust acquisition, jealousy, calumny, and of impiety. I have polluted, corrupted and rendered lewd all my senses and members, in all things fulfilling the will of the Devil. I know, O Lord, that mine iniquities are gone over my head; but thy bounties are immeasurable, thy benignant goodness is unutterable, and there is no sin which can overcome thy love of*

mankind. Wherefore, O King most marvelous, O Lord benign, reveal thy mercies also upon me, a sinner; show forth the power of thy clemency; manifest the might of thine ineffable tenderness of heart, and accept me, a sinner, who now have recourse unto thee. Accept me as thou didst accept the prodigal son, as thou didst accept the thief and the woman who was a sinner. Accept me, who have beyond measure sinned against thee in word, in deed, in unlawful desires and in foolish thoughts. As thou didst receive those who came unto thee at the eleventh hour, and had done nothing worthy, so also receive thou me, a sinner; for I have sinned greatly.

Chapter Eight

FINDING ONE'S TRUE SELF THROUGH SELF-EXAMINATION

St. Andrew of Crete in his famous Canon practices a rigorous self-examination that leads him to embrace repentance as the way to self-knowledge and ultimately union with God.
—Frederica Mathewes-Green*

No man remains quite what he was when he recognizes himself.
—Thomas Mann

We need to be washed clean by the unceasing tears of self-knowledge.
—Alexander Kalomiros

If you put up with yourself, why not put up with everyone else?
—Guigo 1. *Meditations*

---
* *First Fruits of Prayer*. Frederica Mathewes-Green. Paraclete Press, Brewster, MA. 2006.

"SEARCH ME, O GOD"

Let us examine some practical ways by which we can come to know ourselves through self-examination. The psalmist said, "Search me, O God, and know my heart: try me and know my thoughts: and see if there be any wicked way in me, and lead me in the way everlasting" (Psalm 139:23-24). There is a great difference between *my* searching myself and *God's* searching me. When I search myself, the ego defenses will step in to blind me to my false self, but when God searches me through the Holy Spirit and a spiritual mentor, His blinding light will reveal to me a good many things to which I am blind. "Self-knowledge is to be attentive to one's soul," said St. Gregory. Perhaps self-examination is a misnomer since both the Holy Spirit and a spiritual mentor must be involved in true self-examination. The Psalmist's words, "Search me, O God, and know my heart" are vital in attaining self-knowledge.

There is no doubt that knowing oneself through self-examination is a life-long process. Vladimir Lossky said once,

> *Looking into one's soul is like peeling an onion. One began by taking off the outer layers and it was only after some time—perhaps a lifetime—that the inner core could be reached.*

ASCENT TO GOD THROUGH DESCENT INTO ONE'S SELF

"The ascent toward God begins with a descent into oneself," said Paul Evdokimov. "Search me, O God, and know my heart: try me and know my heart...." "If anyone could see his own vices accurately without the veil of self-love, he would worry about nothing else in his life," wrote St. John of the Ladder. Because the burden of our sins can be so oppressive, St. Gregory of Nyssa teaches that God does not allow us to see ourselves in the light of His truth until we are made capable to endure it; otherwise it would horrify us. It requires time, prayer and much effort to know the truth about ourselves, much like Emily Dickinson had in mind when she wrote, "Truth must dazzle gradually or every man be blind."

DAILY EXAMINATION OF CONSCIENCE

An effective way to "know thyself" is through a process of regular examination of conscience with questions such as these:

1) What do I really believe?
2) Who is my real master?
3) For what and for whom do I live?
4) What are my weaknesses, blind spots, shortcomings that I fail to recognize or refuse to acknowledge?
5) What are my highest loyalties?
6) Do I look for scapegoats to blame for my failures?
7) What is my primary purpose, my most important goal in life?
8) Am I wearing a mask, pretending to be someone I am not?
9) What is my destiny?
10) Am I ignoring the ultimate goal of eternal life: to grow and to be what God created me to be?
11) Do I entrust myself to God's love, care and power each day?
12) Do I ask for God's mercy and forgiveness each day?
13) Do I thank God for His blessings each day as I number them one by one?

14) Do I ask God each day for His Holy Spirit to enlighten me to see myself as He sees me?
15) Do I review each day moment by moment, relationship by relationship, focusing on the need for amendment and healing?
16) Do I set aside time each day for silence, prayer and reading God's word, which are effective ways to self-knowledge, since they bring us in touch with the inner self?
17) Do I avail myself of the Sacrament of Confession?

Elder Ephraim stresses the importance of daily self-examination as a means to true self knowledge:

> *Every night, review how you passed the day, and in the morning review how the night passed, so that you know how your soul's accounts are doing. If you see a loss, try to regain it through caution and forcefulness. If you see a profit, glorify God, your invisible helper.**

DAILY SCRUTINY OF THOUGHTS

St. Gregory Palamas suggests that if we scrutinize our thoughts daily by guarding the heart, God will not have to scrutinize us when we appear before Him:

> *Do not leave any part of your soul or body unwatched. In this way you will master the evil spirits that assail you and you will boldly present yourself to Him who examines hearts and minds (cf. Ps. 7:9); and He will not scrutinize you, for you will have already scrutinized yourself. As St. Paul says, "If we judged ourselves we would not be judged" (1 Cor. 11:31).*

---
* Counsels From the Holy Mountain. Elder Ephraim. St. Anthony Greek Orthodox Monastery. Florence, AZ. 1999.

– Chapter Eight –

How can we scrutinize ourselves?

Daily self-examination combined with repentance and confession constitute the best preparation we can make for knowing our true self. Daily scrutiny. Daily self-judgment. Daily repentance.

Another way of scrutinizing ourselves is by reading God's Word each day. God's Word is like a mirror in which we see ourselves as we are and as God wants us to be. Daily scrutiny through self-examination, the reading of God's Word and repentance is how the Christian learns to practice quality control in his life.

In addition to reading the Scriptures, St. Theophan the Recluse emphasized the importance of reading the Church Fathers as an effective means of self-examination:

> *Look to yourself, and have more concern with the heart. To discriminate between movements of the heart, read and reflect on the writings of Sts. John of the Ladder, Isaac of Syria, Barsanouphios and John—also of Diadochos, Philotheos, Abba Isaias, Evagrios, Cassian, and Neilos in the Philokalia; and apply what they say to yourself. When you read, do not just leave impressed on your mind a general idea of the author's argument, but always turn what he says into a personal rule to be applied to yourself. When you do this, the general idea you have formed always undergoes some shades of change.*

St. Hesychios in the *Philokalia* suggests a specific manner of daily self-examination:

> *St. Basil the Great, mouthpiece of Christ and pillar of the Church, says that a great help towards not sinning and not committing daily the same faults is for us to review in our conscience at the end of each day what we have done wrong and what we have done right. Job did this with regard both to himself and to his children (cf. Job 1:5). These daily reckonings illumine a man's hour by hour behaviour.*

THE SOUL'S WINDOW

The eye of the soul is the mind and the heart. These serve as the soul's window through which we come to see and know God and self. It is through the eye of the soul that the light of God's presence shines in us and we are able to see spiritually. But Satan is always working through *logismoi* (thoughts) to darken, obscure and even destroy the eye of the soul, the window to God, so as to prevent us from seeing our true self. He tries to get us to focus our attention on other things which turn out to be false gods or idols. "If your whole eye is sound, your whole body will be full of light" (Matt. 6:2). But "if the light in you is darkness, your whole body will be full of darkness and how great is that darkness," said Jesus.

Through vigilance, prayer and daily self-scrutiny, the spiritual eye must be kept single and pure; for it is through the eye of the soul that we see God and self.

Dee Margaret Pennock encourages daily self-examination to help us discover the sins and passions in us:

> *So a good idea would be not to let a day go by without praying for God to show us the sins and passions that we*

– Chapter Eight –

> haven't yet realized are in us. The great King David used to pray: Who can tell how often we offend? O cleanse me of my secret faults (Ps. 19:12). A useful prayer is: "Lord deliver me from pride and show me the sins I haven't seen. Show me how my sins are acting in me and what they are doing to me."*

> True self-knowledge is to see one's own defects and weaknesses so clearly that they fill our whole view. And mark this—the more you see yourself at fault and deserving of every censure, the more you will advance.
> —St. Theophan the Recluse

FOCUS ON SELF

In order to know one's self, we need to take our eyes off the sins of others and focus on ourselves. But this is not pleasant. In fact, one Englishman called it disgusting. He said, "I think that looking into oneself is disgusting, quite disgusting, not a thing nice people do."

Yet the way to know oneself and to gain theosis is exactly by scrutinizing oneself, looking into oneself critically and with the discernment of the Holy Spirit, as painful as this may be. St. Dorotheos of Gaza spoke to this issue when he wrote,

> Those who want to be saved scrutinize not the shortcomings of their neighbor, but always their own, and they set about eliminating them. Such was the man who saw his brother doing wrong and groaned, "Woe is me; him today—me tomorrow."

---

* *The Adam Complex.* Dee Margaret Pennock. Light and Life Publ. Co., Mpls, MN. 2004.

Carl Jung said once, "Everything that irritates us about others can lead us to an understanding of ourselves."

The following words were found on the tomb of an Anglican bishop (1100 CE) in the crypts of Westminster Abbey:

> *When I was young and free and my imagination had no limits, I dreamed of changing the world. As I grew older and wiser, I discovered the world would not change, so I shortened my sights somewhat and decided to change only my country. But it too seemed immovable. As I grew into my twilight years, on one last desperate attempt, I settled for changing only my family, those closest to me, but alas they would have none of it. And now as I lie on my deathbed, I suddenly realize: If I had only changed myself first, then by example I would have changed my family. From their inspiration and encouragement, I would then have been able to better my country and who knows, I may have even changed the world.*

REVERSE THE BAGS

Abba Poemen said once, "The wickedness of men is hidden behind their backs." He meant that many of us carry two bags: one in front of us where we keep the sins of others, and one just over our shoulders where we can cast our own sins so as not to see them. The Desert Fathers call on us to reverse the bags, i.e., to place our sins in the bag immediately before us and the sins of others in the bag behind us.

"Unable to excuse ourselves," wrote Augustine, "we are ready to accuse others". But there is no salvation in that, only damnation.

– Chapter Eight –

ST. PAUL'S EXPERIENCE

St. Paul practiced this kind of introspection. He did not like what he saw within himself. He wrote about it, "I cannot understand my own behavior," he said. "I fail to carry out the things I want to do, and I find myself doing the very things I hate" (Rom. 7:15). He continues,

> When I act against my will, then, it is not my true self doing it, but sin which lives in me. In fact, this seems to be the rule, that every single time I want to do good it is something evil that comes to hand. In my inmost self I dearly love God's Law, but I can see that my body follows a different law that battles against the law which my reason dictates (Rom. 7:20-23).

Seeing his desperate condition, Paul cried out, "O wretched man that I am! Who will deliver me from this body of death?"

By confronting himself in such a manner, Paul was able to reach out to the Savior to set him free. And he writes joyfully:

> Out of his infinite glory, may he give you the power through his Spirit for your hidden self to grow strong, so that Christ may live in your hearts through faith, and then, planted in love and built on love, you will with all the saints have strength to grasp the breadth and the length, the height and the depth; until, knowing the love of Christ, which is beyond all knowledge, you are filled with the utter fullness of God (Eph. 3:1;6-19).

GOD POPPED HIS BALLOON

The devil is constantly working on us to get us to avoid introspection by getting us to focus on others. An example of this is the person who said,

> *I left church that sunshiny morning feeling a bit smug. The sermon had been a stern attack on the "big three" – alcohol, cigarettes and drugs. The pastor had dwelt on the bad effects these substances had on our bodies, our "temples of the Living Lord". I could be smug. I was a non-smoker, non-drinker, who had never touched hard drugs, and I felt a benign kind of pity for those who had.*
>
> *And then the Lord, as He so frequently does, popped my balloon. He reminded me in clear "instant replays" of those times in my life when I had been "drunk" with the pride of overcoming these awful temptations; "smoking" over the way I'd been slighted by a busy salesclerk; "high" over the misfortune of someone I had no use for because it served him right. He reminded me of the times when I had "hangovers" of depression when life didn't give me what I thought I deserved, when I'd "spaced out" trying to emulate a group I thought had the answers, but weren't God-centered; when I had been "burned up" over tasks my children had left undone after I had assigned them.*
>
> *A quiet voice seemed to say, "Shall I go on?"*
>
> *Contritely I replied, "No, thanks. I've got the message."*

– Chapter Eight –

"EICHMANN IS IN ALL OF US"

Adolph Eichmann was one of the worst of the Holocaust masterminds. When he stood trial, prosecutors called a string of former concentration camp prisoners as witnesses. One was a small haggard man named Yehiel Dinur, who had miraculously escaped death in Auschwitz.

On his day to testify, Dinur entered the courtroom and stared at the man behind the bulletproof glass—the man who had presided over the slaughter of millions. As the eyes of the two men met—victim and murderous tyrant—the courtroom fell silent, filled with the tension of the confrontation.

Then suddenly, Yehiel Dinur began to sob, collapsing to the floor. Was he overcome by hatred…by the horrifying memories…by the evil incarnate in Eichmann's face?

No. As he later explained in an interview, it was because Eichmann was not the demonic personification of evil Dinur had expected. Rather, he was an ordinary man, just like anyone else. And in that one instant, Dinur came to the stunning realization that sin and evil are the human condition. "I was afraid about myself," Dinur said. "I saw that I am capable to do this…exactly like he."

Dinur's shocking conclusion? "Eichmann is in all of us."

For people to see their need for a Savior, they must first see the truth about themselves as St. Paul did when he called himself "the chief of sinners".

The Nun Magdalina wrote,

> *Why do we criticize others? Because we do not try to know ourselves. Whoever is busy trying to know himself has no time to notice the faults of others. Judge yourself and you will stop judging others. Regard every man as better than you are, for without this thought a man is far from God, even though he performs miracles.*

The words of St. John the Dwarf need to be heard:

> *We have put the light burden aside, that is, self-accusation; and we have loaded ourselves with a heavy burden, that is, self-justification. Humility and the fear of God are above all virtues.*

Socrates said that the unexamined life is not worth living. An unbeliever added that the examined life makes you wish you were dead. Not so, however, if one examines oneself in the presence of the merciful God Who can forgive and lead to newness of life.

THE DANGER OF SELF-KNOWLEDGE WITHOUT CHRIST

Self-knowledge without Christ can lead to great despair. Fulton Sheen brought this out when he wrote,

> *Atheists shudder at the prospect of going down into the pit of their real selves, for there is no exit for them toward happiness. Not having the humility to face the fact that their real selves are guilty, they deny the very existence of guilt, although seeing their sins would be the essential condition of their cure. Self knowledge is never*

― Chapter Eight ―

despairing to those who acknowledge the power of God. Who fears to reveal sickness to a physician who can cure him? Who fears to reveal his guilt to a Savior Who redeems? Self-examination to the Christian is the digging of a foundation. The deeper the foundation, the higher the building will finally soar. The more humble the soul, the greater will be his exaltation when God touches him.*

Do not let the eye of the mind turn away from the heart; and when anything comes forth from there, at once catch it and examine it. If it is good, let it be; if it is not good, it must be killed at once. In this way, learn to know yourself. If some thought emerges more often than others, it signifies a passion stronger than the rest. This means that you must combat it with greater energy. Yet do not place any reliance on yourself and do not expect to achieve anything by your own efforts. All means of healing and all remedies are sent by the Lord. So give yourself up to Him—and this at all times. Strive and go on striving; but expect all good to come only from the Lord.
—Theophan the Recluse

---

* *On Being Human.* Fulton Sheen. Doubleday, Garden City, NY. 1982.

Chapter Nine

FINDING ONE'S TRUE SELF THROUGH INNER STILLNESS

Solitude is the furnace of transformation. Without solitude we remain victims of our society and continue to be entangled in the illusions of the false self.... Solitude is the place of the great struggle and the great encounter—the struggle against the compulsions of the false self, and the encounter with the loving God who offers himself as the substance of the new self.

—Henri Nouwen

– Chapter Nine –

STILLNESS

Still another way to come to know oneself is through stillness.

Ernest Cardenal said once,

> *Modern man always tries to flee from himself. He can never be silent or alone, because that would mean to be alone with himself, and this is why the places of amusement and the cinemas are always filled with people. And when they find themselves alone and are at a point where they might encounter God, they turn on the radio or the television set.**

If we can't be quiet, we cannot hear the inner voice of God speaking to us. Before Jesus began His public ministry, he retired to the wilderness to be alone with God. "Jesus was led by the Spirit out into the wilderness to be tempted by the devil" (Matthew 4:1). It was there in the wilderness that Jesus had to confront the issue of Himself. Who was He? What kind of a Savior was He to be? The devil tempted Him to be a political Messiah with its privileges of wealth, power and fame. But Jesus refused. He chose instead total dependence on God, humility and obedience to God's will. He chose to reject the false self the devil was trying to impose on Him. He chose to be the humble, self-sacrificing Messiah the Father wanted Him to be.

The Spirit led Jesus to the wilderness. It was there that, humanly speaking, He was able to introspect, to look into Himself and establish His identity as to the kind of Messiah He was to be.

---

* *"To Live is to Love"*. Herder and Herder. 1972.

THE STILLNESS OF SELF-KNOWLEDGE

The Desert Fathers tell the story of three brothers who wanted to know how best to serve God. They went to see a monk for advice. He acted out a little parable. He took a jug of water and poured the water into a bowl. Then he made them look into it. The surface of the water was all murky and ruffled, and they could see nothing. A few minutes later, he made them look into it again. This time the surface was crystal clear and smooth. Looking into it, they could see their faces reflected. So, he explained, unless you become quiet, tranquil, you cannot come to see and know yourself. You cannot see your faults nor will you be able to see the image of God that abides in the depth of your being.

As long as there are ripples on the surface, nothing can be reflected properly. As long as the mud at the bottom of the pond has not settled, the vision will be murky. These analogies apply to the state of the human heart. "Blessed are the pure in heart for they shall see God" (Matt. 5:8).

"If a man cannot be alone, he doesn't know who he is," said Thomas Merton.

When you are completely alone with God, sitting in His presence in holy silence, you will be able to see clearly your image in the mirror of God. It is in this silence that you will see your many shortcomings. It is here that you will find, as well, a chance to entreat God and weep, that your tears may wash away your sins and make you whiter than snow. "In quietness and in confidence shall be your strength" (Is. 30:15). "Nothing is better than to realize one's weakness, and nothing is worse than not to be aware of it" (Peter of Damascus, 12th century).

– Chapter Nine –

A SPIRITUAL FATHER OR MENTOR

The Orthodox spiritual tradition, as we have seen, places great emphasis on the need for a spiritual mentor in the process of knowing oneself. St. Basil, for example, wrote in his *The Greater Rules:* "It is difficult for solitaries to discover their faults. They do not have anyone to point them out. They have no one to correct them.... The person not living in community will find neither reproof nor improvement."

When a young novice enters an Orthodox monastery, he is asked to appear before his spiritual Father each evening to manifest his thoughts. This daily encounter with oneself and one's thoughts through a spiritual father is very demanding, but it leads to spiritual growth in knowing oneself, leading to repentance and greater self-knowledge. "Make yourself known to a spiritual Father or mentor and you will come to know yourself. I found my identity more by being known than by knowing myself," said one struggling Christian.

The hesychastic Fathers, like St. Paul, affirmed and taught that man is a Temple of the Holy Spirit. God is present within. What is needed is inner attentiveness to the Holy Spirit Who is constantly speaking within our hearts of the Father's infinite love for us. For this they teach the necessity of inner stillness, *hesychia*, or resting in active self-surrender to God's love. For inner silence is not negative. It is listening actively to the voice of God speaking within us.

We come to self-knowledge through stillness and silence, through attentiveness and *nepsis*. Abba Bessarion, at the point of death, said, "The monk ought to be as the cherubim: all eye." Having withdrawn to the desert, Abba Arsenius heard a voice saying to him, "Arsenius, flee; *be silent*; pray always. These are the sources of sinlessness."

St. Symeon said of Moses, "Moses went up to the mountain as a mere man; he came down carrying God with him." St. Anthony went into the desert a mere man. He came out of it carrying God. So did the other saints. So can we if we daily descend with the mind into the heart, there to stand in God's presence. We will come away with a greater knowledge of God and self.

A brother once came to visit Abba Moses and asked him for a word of advice. The old man said to him, "Go, sit in your cell and your cell will teach you everything."

GREAT DISCOVERIES MADE IN SILENCE

It is in silence that some of the world's greatest discoveries have been made. Archimedes discovered the law of specific gravity while relaxing in silence in his bath. Galileo discovered the principle of the pendulum while praying silently in the cathedral of Pisa. When the scientist of today would wrest some secret of nature's mystery, he does not set up his apparatus in the midst of a noisy and crowded street, but in some quiet and remote laboratory, where he waits for nature to speak. It is so when man waits for God to speak. He must close the door on the world.

Yet, we fear silence, so we surround ourselves with noise. We are afraid of what silence brings. It makes us pay attention to ourselves, revealing the thoughts of our hearts. Fearing this, we flee. Yet it is through silence that we may enter God's presence and come to grips with who we are.

— Chapter Nine —

"BE STILL AND KNOW..."

"Be still and know that I am God," says the Lord. Be still! Stop your rushing about all tensed up, acting as if everything depends on you, acting as if you are God. Stop! "Be still and know that I am God." In stillness as we practice God's presence, we discover who God is and who we are. The noises and disturbances of the world serve to hide our faults and our true selves from us. The Desert Fathers were disciples of Jesus in honest search for their true selves in Christ.

"Silence. All human unhappiness comes from not knowing how to stay quietly in a room," said Pascal.

GOD CREATES SILENCES FOR US

God makes silences in every life; the silence of sleep, the silence of sickness, the silence of sorrow, and then the last great silence of death. One of the hardest things in the world is to get little children to keep still. They are in a state of perpetual activity, restless, eager, questioning, alert. And just as mother says to her child, "Be still," and hushes it to sleep that it may rest, so God does sooner or later with all of us. What a quiet, still place the sick-room is! What a time for self-examination! What silence there is in a house where a loved one has died! How the voices are hushed, and every footstep soft. Had we the choosing of our own affairs we would never have chosen such an hour as that; and yet how often it is rich in blessing. All the activities of our years may not have taught us quite so much as we learned in the silences of sickness, sorrow and death. So God comes, in his irresistible way, which never ceases to be a way of love, and says, "Be still, and know that I am God."

The great psychologist William James said once that being alone with God in prayer is much like the experience of a person who, being jostled in a crowd, climbs on a nearby doorstep, looks over the heads of the people, sees what the crowd as a whole is doing, and is then able to descend again into the jam and push; this time, not in the direction the crowd is traveling but *in the right direction.* Like a person in a telephone booth with the door open, we are bombarded daily by the many conflicting voices of the crowd. What we need is to close the door on the crowd daily and listen to the voice of God Who is trying so hard to speak to us.

In the words of the late Henri Nouwen,

> *Solitude is the furnace of transformation. Without solitude we remain victims of our society and continue to be entangled in the illusions of the false self.... Solitude is the place of the great struggle and the great encounter—the struggle against the compulsions of the false self, and the encounter with the loving God who offers himself as the substance of the new self.*

Chapter Ten

FINDING ONE'S TRUE SELF THROUGH THE HOLY SPIRIT

> We can never see the state of our soul in all its nakedness...without the special grace and help of God, because the interior of our soul is always hidden from us by our self-love, prejudices, passions, worldly cares, delusions.
>
> —St. Innocent of Alaska,
> *Indication Of the Way into the Kingdom of Heaven*

THE ROLE OF THE HOLY SPIRIT IN SELF-KNOWLEDGE

No one can truly know oneself without the Holy Spirit. St. Isaac the Syrian wrote, "The perception of man's sins is a gift which comes from God." We do not repent solely on our own effort. It is a gift of the Holy Spirit. Metropolitan Innocent of Moscow emphasized this when he wrote:

> *However intelligent, sensible, and clever a man may be, if he does not possess the Holy Spirit within him, he cannot know himself properly; for without God's help he cannot see the inner state of his soul. But when the Holy Spirit enters the heart of man, he shows him all his inner poverty and weakness, the corruption of his soul and heart, and his remoteness from God.**

Archimandrite Sophrony added, "Sin is recognized by the gift of the Holy Spirit combined with faith in the Personal Absolute, our Creator and Father." Only the Holy Spirit can fathom the depths of the human heart and know it fully.

Thus, to achieve self-knowledge we need to bring every thought entering our mind "into captivity to the obedience of Christ" (2 Cor. 10:5). We need to submit at each moment every thought to God's Spirit dwelling within us, ever conscious of His presence within us as we place each thought under the sign of Christ.

God's word tells us that (1) the Holy Spirit directs and controls my life; (2) the Holy Spirit teaches me everything; (3) the Holy Spirit leads me to all truth. As Jesus says,

---

* *The Art of Prayer*. Chariton. Faber and Faber. London. 1966.

– Chapter Ten –

I have much more to tell you, but now it would be too much for you to bear. When, however, the spirit comes, who reveals the truth about God, he will lead you into all the truth. He will not speak on his own authority, but he will speak of what he hears and will tell you of things to come. He will give me glory, because he will take what I say and tell it to you. All that my Father has is mine; that is why I said that the Spirit will take what I give him and tell it to you.
—John 16:12-15

The Holy Spirit has already revealed who we are after we put on Christ in holy baptism:
- I am beautiful to God – Isaiah 61:10
- I am blessed – Jer. 17:7
- I am the salt of the earth – Matt. 5:13
- I am the light of the world – Matt. 5:14
- I am God's child – John 1:12
- I have eternal life – John 6:47
- I am Christ's friend – John 15:15
- I am chosen to bear fruit – John 15:16
- I am forever free from condemnation – Rom. 8:1
- I am an heir of God – Rom. 8:17
- I cannot be separated from God's love – Rom. 8:35
- I am gifted – Rom. 12:6
- I am full of hope – Rom. 15:13
- I am in Christ – 1 Cor. 1:30
- I am a temple of the living God – 1 Cor. 3:16; 6:19
- I am bought with a price – 1 Cor. 6:20
- I belong to God – 1 Cor. 6:20
- I am a member of Christ's body – 1 Cor. 12:27
- I am a new creation – 2 Cor. 5:17
- I am a minister of reconciliation – 2 Cor. 5:20

- I am God's co-worker – 2 Cor. 6:1
- I am crucified with Christ – Gal. 2:20
- I am alive in Christ – Gal. 2:20
- I am a saint – Eph. 1:1
- I am blessed with every spiritual blessing – Eph. 1:3
- I am being saved – Eph. 2:5-9
- I am seated with Christ in heavenly places – Eph. 2:6
- I am God's workmanship – Eph. 2:10
- I am becoming mature in Christ – Eph. 4:13
- I am filled with the Spirit – Eph. 5:18
- I am strong in the Lord – Eph. 6:10
- I am empowered to obey God – Phil. 2:13
- I can do all things through Christ who strengthens me – Phil. 4:13
- I am honored – 2 Tim. 2:21
- I have a high priest who sympathizes with me in all my weaknesses – Heb. 4:15
- I can find grace and mercy to help in time of need – Heb. 4:16
- I am holy – Heb. 10:10
- I am a royal priest – 1 Peter 2:9
- I am a partaker of the divine nature – 2 Peter 1:4

BAPTISM AND OUR IDENTITY

Christ restores our lost sense of identity. He calls us into His royal family. He did this in baptism when we were chrismated and first received the Eucharist. Those who have put on Christ in holy baptism have a totally new theological identity. Thus, as Orthodox Christians we do not have to wrestle with our identity as many people do today. Why? Because our identity was given to us in baptism when God said about each one of us: "You are my beloved son/daughter in whom I am well pleased." It is time then that we who have been baptized into Christ stop rummaging for our identity in Eastern religions as well as in the garbage heaps of this world and begin to claim the treasure we received in holy baptism. We have our identity! "We are God's children now," writes St. John. St. Paul says that God "has *blessed us* in Christ ...has *chosen us* in Him before the foundation of the world ...*destined us* in love to be His sons and daughters through Christ Jesus ...*appointed (us)* to live for the praise of His glory ...*sealed (us)* with the promised Holy Spirit." This is our true identity in Christ, which we need to claim and to live.

> *The person who listens to Christ fills himself with light, and if he imitates Christ, he reclaims himself.*
> —St. Thalassios the Libyan

We need to reclaim the new self (identity) we received in baptism through daily repentance, for repentance is not just feeling sorry for wrongs we have done; it is, even more so, an invitation to reclaim the new life we received in baptism. We die to sin in order to be alive to God (Rom. 6:11). We need to become who we are, claiming and nurturing the new life we received in holy baptism.

> *You have stripped off your old behavior with your old self, and you have put on a new self...renewed in the image of its Creator (Col. 3:10-11).*

> *...by the complete stripping of your natural self...you have been buried with him by your baptism. (Col. 2:11-12)*

NOT THROUGH YOGA OR EASTERN RELIGIONS

A word must be said at this point about seeking to find one's self in yoga and eastern meditation. It cannot be emphasized sufficiently that such means actually serve to render us blind to the inner self. Through yoga we avoid all too easily seeing the true self, that is, the sinner, and instead are lead into a process of self-deification. Orthodox Christianity teaches us that even though we are created in the image of God, we can never approach the "essence" of God, but can become by grace "gods by adoption", adopted by God and made "partakers of divine nature". It is only in Christ and through the grace of the Holy Spirit that God can reveal our true self to us.

To help us see ourselves as we truly are, we need the Holy Spirit Who comes to us especially through prayer—the key that opens the door to self-knowledge.

> *Prayer is a spiritual barometer for self-observation. Just as a barometer shows us how heavy or light the air is, so prayer shows us how high or low our spirit has gone in its relationship to God.*
> —St. Theophan the Recluse (1815-1894)

– Chapter Eleven –

Chapter Eleven

FINDING ONE'S TRUE SELF THROUGH HUMILITY

The farther a man knows himself to be from perfection, the nearer he is to it.
—Gerard Groote

The most profound and valuable lesson of all is to truly know yourself and to have a humble opinion of yourself.
—Thomas à Kempis

THE ROLE OF HUMILITY IN SELF KNOWLEDGE

St. Isaac described the role of humility in self-knowledge as follows,

> *The person who has attained the knowledge of his own weakness has reached the summit of humility.*

Humility re-centers life in the Person of Jesus in Whom through repentance we find our true identity. For, repentance must be understood not simply as a negation of our false self but also, and even more so, as discovering and receiving the gift of a new identity even as Abram became Abraham (Gen. 17:5); Jacob became Israel (Gen. 32:30); Simon became Peter (Matt. 16:18) and Saul became Paul (Acts 13:9).

Humility, then, as one of the fruits of self-knowledge and repentance, is a letting go of one's false self, a self-surrender that leads ultimately to the death of selfishness. It is this spirit-born humility, says Augustine, that can destroy what he calls the "lust of vindicating ourselves".

HUMILITY: THE DOORWAY TO TRUTH

The doorway to humility is acknowledging and then accepting the truth. For, humility is simply admitting what is true. It is the dissolution of all pretense, a commitment to honesty and authenticity. It is truth that liberates and sets us free. Born of humility and repentance, self-knowledge is the way to liberation and joy.

– Chapter Eleven –

A saint of the Western Church, Vincent DePaul (1576-1660), put it this way, "the reason why God is so great a lover of humility is because He is the great lover of truth. Now humility is nothing but truth, whereas pride is nothing but lying."

> *Keep both eyes open. This is the measure of humility: if a man is humble he never thinks that he has been treated worse than he deserves. He stands so low in his own estimation that no one, however hard they try, can think more poorly of him than he thinks himself. This is the whole secret of the matter.*
> —St. Theophan the Recluse

> *The Lord sometimes leaves in us some defects of character in order that we should learn humility. For without them we would immediately soar above the clouds in our own estimation and would place our throne there. And herein lies perdition.*
> —St. Theophan the Recluse

> *Humility is the greatest of all virtues. If as a result of sincere repentance it is planted in you, you will also be given the gift of prayer and self-control, and you will be freed from servitude to the passions.*
> —Nikitas Stithatos

> *A humble understanding of ourselves is a more certain way to God than the most in-depth study.*
> —Thomas à Kempis

We must beware of thinking either too highly or too lowly of ourselves. One leads to pride and the other to despair. God wants us to see ourselves as we truly are. Romans 12:3 says,

"Do not think of yourself more highly than you ought, but rather think of yourself with sober judgment, in accordance with the measure of faith God has given you." To become what we are meant to be, we must come to know ourselves as God knows us.

Our true self must increase, our false self must decrease. "I must decrease, He (Jesus) must increase" (St. John the Baptist).

To accomplish this, God often allows us to experience "little falls" as de Caussade explains, "Little falls are permitted in order to help us practice humility and patience and to accept ourselves. Such falls are far more useful to us than victories that are spoiled by vain complacency."

These "little falls" have been called the "cracks" in life: they allow the light to seep in so that we may know ourselves as totally dependent on God. As the line in a Leonard Cohan song says, "Forget your perfect offering. There is a crack in everything. That's how the light gets in." It is the "cracks" in life that expose our brokenness and reveal the self as fallible and dependent on God.

> When a ray of sunlight enters the house through a crack, it lights up everything inside and even shows up the finest dust in its beam. So it is with the fear of the Lord, when it enters a human heart, it reveals all the fallibility still lurking there.
> —John Climacus

St. Paul spoke of such "cracks" in his life that served to let in God's light:

– Chapter Eleven –

"And lest I should be exalted above measure through the abundance of the revelations, there was given to me a thorn in the flesh, the messenger of Satan to buffet me lest I should be exalted above measure."

> For this thing I besought the Lord three times, that it might depart from me. And he said, My grace is sufficient for you; for my strength is made perfect in weakness (2 Cor. 12:7-9).
>
> 'Know thyself': this is true humility, the humility that teaches us to be inwardly humble and makes our heart contrite. Such humility you must cultivate and guard. For if you do not yet know yourself you cannot know what humility is, and have not yet embarked truly on the task of cultivating and guarding. To know oneself is the goal of the practice of the virtues.
> —Nikitas Stithatos

Lawrence Scopoli points to distrust of self as a way to self-knowledge:

> We easily overstimate our own abilities. It is not easy to spot the error in this.
>
> Distrust of our own strength is a gift from heaven. Sometimes we receive it through the inspiration of God. Sometimes it arrives with afflictions and overwhelming temptations.
>
> There are four things we need to do if we would gain this spiritually healthy distrust of ourselves.

Meditate upon our own weakness. Admit that we cannot accomplish the smallest good without God's help.

Beg God for what God alone can give. Acknowledge that we don't have it, and that we can't go somewhere and get it. Let's fall down at the feet of our Lord and plead with him to grant our request.

Gradually discard the illusions of our own mind, our tendency to sin, and begin to see the overwhelming, yet hidden, obstacles that surround us.

As often as we commit a fault, we must take inventory of our weaknesses. God permits us to fall only in order to help us gain deeper insight into ourselves.

God permits us to sin more or less grievously in proportion to our pride. Every time we commit a fault, we should earnestly ask God to enlighten us. Ask him to help you see yourself as you are in his sight.

Presume no more on your own strength. Otherwise, you will stumble again over the same stone.
—Lawrence Scupoli: *The Spiritual Combat*

Chapter Twelve

FINDING ONE'S TRUE SELF THROUGH REPENTANCE AND THE RENUNCIATION OF EVIL

Repentance doesn't mean feeling bad about yourself, guilty and miserable. It is seeing the truth: admitting the truth about yourself, and the truth about God, which is that He already knew this truth about you and loves you anyway.*

—Frederica Mathewes-Green

---

* *First Fruits of Prayer.* Frederica Mathewes-Green. Paraclete Press, Brewster, MA. 2006.

DISCOVERING OURSELVES

Repentance and confession constitute a way of rediscovering ourselves. This is so because repentance removes sin which blinds us to our true self. Through repentance the eye of the soul is purified, enabling us to see our true self, the image of God in us.

Man finds his true self in the image of the One in whose likeness he was created: Jesus. Because man's relationship to God has been ruptured by sin, man must come to see himself as a sinner and plead God's mercy before he can know God. The image of God marred by sin, must be repaired, renewed, restored.

Knowledge of God, then, begins with knowledge of self. It begins with knowledge of our sinfulness and a cry for God's mercy. "Lord, be merciful to me the sinner."

THE PRODIGAL SON CAME TO HIMSELF

In his badness, the Prodigal Son had no understanding of himself and of what he was doing, but when he repented and said of himself with a frank and merciless honesty, renouncing self-excuse, self-pity, self-defense, "I have sinned," then it was that he saw the evil in himself. And as soon as he said, "I have sinned," he resolved, "I will arise and go to my father." And this is exactly what Jesus urges. When we see ourselves for what we truly are, are ashamed of ourselves, have difficulty accepting ourselves, we can be certain of one thing—God will accept us. About nothing is Jesus more emphatic. He will deliver us from the chains of self-pity, self-excuse, self-justification and empower us to live in Christ and for Christ.

— Chapter Twelve —

That is why Jean Pierre de Caussade said once, "Rejoice every time you can discover a new imperfection." That imperfection can lead you to repentance and to newness of life in Christ.

"FATHER, YOU DO NOT HAVE SUCH SINS!"

Abba Dioscorus was once found weeping. When asked why he was weeping, Dioscorus replied, "I am weeping for my sins." The young fellow-monk knew that Dioscorus had always endeavored to live a holy life, so he said to him, "Father, you do not have such sins." Dioscorus replied, "Truly, my child, if I were allowed to see my sins, three or four men would not be enough to weep for them."

St. Andrew of Crete felt the same about his sinfulness. Witness the sorrow he expressed in his penitential *Canon of St. Andrew of Crete*:

More than all have I sinned;
I alone have sinned against You.
O God my Savior,
have compassion upon me, Your creature.

> *There has never been a sin, a deed, an evil act,*
> *which I have not cherished, O Savior.*
> *I have sinned in thoughts, words and deeds,*
> *and no one has sinned more than I.*
>
> *David was a forefather of the Lord, O my soul,*
> *yet he sinned doubly by committing both*
> *murder and adultery.*
> *Your sickness, however, is even worse than his deeds*
> *because of your impulsive will.*

*David, though once compounding his sins
by first murdering a man and then stealing his wife,
was quick to repent of both.
You, however, O my soul, have done worse things than
he, yet you never repented of them before God.*

*I have sinned, Lord, I have sinned against You.
Be merciful to me
though there is no one whose sins I have not surpassed.*

Both Abba Dioscorus and St. Andrew of Crete demonstrate that the first step to self-knowledge is to take a good hard look at the inner cleansing that needs to take place.

COMPUNCTION IS NOT DEGRADING ONESELF

Such an attitude of compunction is not degrading; it is correct diagnosis. It is not judgmentalism, because the judgment is the same for all of us, since we have all sinned and fallen short of God's glory. It is not false guilt because much of the guilt we face is real guilt; guilt that we deserve. It is such guilt that is designed by God to bring us to the source of healing and renewal, the source of our true identity in Christ Jesus. For, truly, as Martin Buber said once, "If a man will not judge himself, all things judge him, and all things become messengers of God." Thus, in the words of Thomas Carlyle, "The greatest of all faults is to be conscious of none."

CONFRONT YOUR WEAKNESSES

To know ourselves, we need to confront our weaknesses. St. Isaac said, "Blessed is the person who knows his own weakness, because this knowledge becomes for him the foundation and

– Chapter Twelve –

the beginning of all that is good and beautiful." To know ourselves as we truly are, warts and all, is to see ourselves without delusions, says St. Isaac. And this is the beginning of holiness; the beginning of repentance and newness of life in Christ. For, in the words of Pascal, "Unless we know ourselves to be full of pride, ambition, concupiscence, weakness, wretchedness and unrighteousness, we are truly blind." Tito Colliander expressed it this way, "Only when you have seen your imperfection, can you be perfected. Thus perfection proceeds out of weakness."*

THE BEGINNING OF WISDOM

If we know God, we will know ourselves. And if we truly know ourselves we will be humble and fear God; this is the beginning of wisdom and the opposite of pride. Knowing our imperfections, however, without this knowledge of God, is dangerous and can lead to despair. It is essential, therefore, that we know both ourselves (our sins, weaknesses and faults) as well as God. Pascal brought this out when he wrote these classic lines:

> *Knowing God without knowing our own wretchedness makes for pride.*
>
> *Knowing our own wretchedness without knowing God makes for despair*
>
> *Knowing Jesus Christ strikes the balance because he shows us both God and our own wretchedness.*
> —Pensees

---

* *Way of the Ascetics.* Tito Colliander, SVS Press, Crestwood, NY. 1960.

GOD DOES NOT REVEAL OUR SINS TO US UNTIL WE ARE READY

It was stated previously that St. John of Kronstadt (19th century) believed that God does not reveal our imperfections and sins to us unless He can see in us sufficient faith, fortitude and hope for us not to be broken by the revelation of our sins. When He does reveal these faults to us, we can rejoice in the knowledge that God has seen enough faith and hope in us to allow us by His grace to cope with these sins. We can, therefore, rejoice that God has granted us His trust. He believes that we can now take the necessary steps to repentance, self knowledge and newness of life.

Dr. M. Scott Peck, author of the book *The Road Less Traveled*, wrote, "Evil is the persistent refusal of the evil person to face the truth about himself. He is constantly scapegoating, laying it on other people, projecting his sins onto others." If some of us get the idea that we are without sin, not only will we never repent but our passions will enslave us and lead us to destruction.

> *Self-justification is when a man denies his sin, as we see in the case of Adam, even, Cain and others who have sinned but, wishing to justify themselves, denied their sin.*
> —Barsanuphius

UNCOVERING THE EVIL IN US

There is much evil in each one of us. Our great problem is that we are blind to it. To know ourselves spiritually we have to confront the evil within us. Self-discovery is a continuing task we must all undertake. There is a great deal of evil in the human heart, a great deal of wickedness which motivates much of our lives. We cannot truly know ourselves unless we uncover and remove this evil in us. Evil is not just out there lying on the street or in the gutter. It is in human hearts. In people! In us!

Confronting and eradicating the evil in us involves a life-long struggle of ascesis. St. Macarius the Great emphasizes that while it is incumbent upon us to fight evil, only God can uproot it:

> The uprooting of sin and the evil that is so embedded in our sinning can be done only by divine power. For it is impossible and outside man's competence to uproot sin. To struggle, yes, to continue to fight, to inflict blows and to receive setbacks is in your power. To uproot, however, belongs to God alone. If, indeed, you could have done it on your own, what would have been the need for the coming of the Lord?
> —St. Macarius the Great, Homilies 3.3,4, in Spiritual Homilies

Kenneth L. Bakken advises us to consider that the journey to self-discovery is also the way to theosis:

> The journey toward wholeness—the way of theosis—is a journey of self-discovery. As we become more aware of our inner selves, we are likely to encounter repulsive, even horrifying images during prayer and meditation. These "inner demons" arise from unhealed wounds, and should be articulated, healed, and integrated. As Walter Wink states, "Traditional Christian pietism has done little to help us embrace these inner demons. It has either denied their reality and projected the evil out on others,

whom it has then 'demonized' (Communists, adulterers, homosexuals), or it has demonized the very emotions themselves, naming and 'casting out' a Spirit of Anger, a Spirit of Envy, or a Spirit of Lust. Neither solution acknowledges this evil as our own."...

A world view that acknowledges the reality of evil cannot be dismissed as premodern. We must take seriously the ancient baptismal rite: renouncing all the forces of evil, the devil, and powers that rebel against God. We must trust in Christ's victory that brings forgiveness, freedom, and a joyful, abundant life.*

"For our struggle is not against enemies of flesh and blood, but against the rulers, against the authorities, against the cosmic powers of this present darkness, against the spiritual forces of evil in the heavenly places" (Eph. 6:12).

---

* *The Journey Into God.* Kenneth L. Bakken. Augsburg Publ. Co. Mpls, MN 2000.

Chapter Thirteen

FINDING ONE'S TRUE SELF BY RENOUNCING PRIDE

Our problem is that the actual condition of our spiritual sickness is hidden from us under a thick mantle of self-love and passions. Only occasionally, thanks to our conscience, do we get a glimpse of our major and most obvious spiritual wounds.
—St. Innocent, Metropolitan of Moscow

We discover meaning and purpose not in the search for self, but in surrender of self, in obedience to Christ. In right relationship to our Creator, knowing we belong to Him, we pour ourselves out in service to others.
—Anonymous

A BALANCED VIEW OF OURSELVES

An elderly minister, a Boy Scout, and a science professor were the only passengers on a small plane. As they were flying, the engine began making strange noises. The pilot left the controls and told the passengers, "This plane is going down. We only have three parachutes, and there are four of us. I must have a parachute, for I have a wife and small children who need me." He grabbed a packet, strapped it to his back, and jumped.

That left three people with only two parachutes. The science professor leaped to his feet and said, "I absolutely must have a parachute. I am the smartest man in the world. My work benefits the whole human race. Humanity needs me." The scientist grabbed a packet, strapped it to his back, and jumped.

That left the elderly preacher and the Boy Scout. The old pastor looked at the boy and said, "I'm not eager to die, but I've had a full life and I'm ready to meet God. You're young, and I want you to go on living. Here, you take the last parachute, and I'll go down with the plane."

The boy replied, "Relax, Reverend. We still have two parachutes left. The smartest man in the world just jumped out of the plane with my backpack."

Many of us enjoy jokes like this because we don't like people who think too highly of themselves, especially one who brags that he is "the smartest person in the world". It has been said that "pride is the only disease known to man that makes everyone sick except the one who has it."

– Chapter Thirteen –

It is true that some people think too highly of themselves but many of us have the opposite problem. We have a very low opinion of ourselves. Certainly God does not want His children to feel inferior, especially when He has lavished so many gifts upon us. Self-knowledge begins with a sound spiritual evaluation. That is why St. Paul says, "Think of yourself with sober judgment, in accordance with the measure of faith God has given you" (Romans 12:3).

KNOW THAT YOU ARE NOT GOD

The words, "Know thyself" mean to know the truth about yourself, i.e., to know that you are a creature and not God and that you are not to transgress the human limits. Abraham Heschel elaborated on this when he wrote,

> *The maxim "know thyself" which was inscribed at the gate of the Temple of Apollo at Delphi referred to self-knowledge in relation to the gods.... (It meant) "Know that you are human and nothing more"*—a warning against presumption, and a call to ... temperance.*

When God told Adam and Eve not to eat of the tree of good and evil, we need to remember that the phrase "good and evil" as it is used in this story is a Hebrew expression that means "everything". Thus it was the tree of "knowing everything". In telling them not to eat of the fruit of this tree, God was telling Adam and Eve to refrain from trying to be "know-it-alls". He was telling them that they could fulfill their place in creation by accepting their human limitations, i.e., their creaturehood, and not to try to be like the Creator, Who is the one and only "know-it-all", i.e., the Omniscient One. God was telling them that to try to take the place of the Creator would destroy them.

* *Who is Man.* Abraham Heschel.

While Greek philosophy taught "know thyself", Jesus came to teach us that it is only by losing oneself in God that we can find life and true self-knowledge. I like the words attributed to columnist Ann Landers who once said humorously, "Know yourself. Don't accept your dog's admiration as conclusive evidence that you are wonderful."

THE CURE FOR PRIDE

The Desert Fathers tell of a younger brother who asked an elder, "What shall I do? I am tempted by pride." The elder responded, "You are right to be proud. Was it not you who made heaven and earth?" With these few words, the brother was cured of pride. He had to be made aware that he was a creature not the Creator. "Know thyself" is not possible without coming to know ourselves as God's estranged children who need to be restored to their original relationship with their Creator, their Father in heaven.

We lack self-knowledge because of pride. Lactantius wrote of the early pagans (4th century):

> *This is the cause of their perverseness, namely ignorance of themselves; and if anyone, having gained the knowledge of the truth, shall have shaken off this ignorance, he will know to what object his life is to be directed, and how it is to be spent.*

HOW PRIDE ATTACKS THE MIND

Dee Margaret Pennock describes how pride attacks the mind,

Chapter Thirteen

> *The passion of pride disables our thinking power. It makes us ignorant of things we'd know if we didn't have that passion—like who God is, and who and what we are, essential knowledge that we need in order to know exactly how to live....*
>
> *From not knowing who God is and who we are, we get ourselves mixed up with God (and even with other people, and with characters who are figments of our imagination). We imagine we can do things only God can do, like making people love one another. We think we can run the world, and our cities and families and everything, by ourselves, without God. Some people fantasize that they can re-create God's world like Karl Marx, who said, I will reduce the world to ashes and then stride through the wreckage a creator.**

Pride is self-ignorance. You think you are God when you are not. Pennock suggests that we fight pride by praying the 51st Psalm each day and saying, "Lord, deliver me from pride and give me self-knowledge."

The most serious obstacle to reaching the truth about oneself is pride or self-love which focuses constantly on self. It makes a person miserable. It is only as I forget self and focus on God and others that I begin to discover who I am.

St. Innocent, Metropolitan of Moscow, put it this way,

> *Our problem is that the actual condition of our spiritual sickness is hidden from us under a thick mantle of self-love and passions. Only occasionally, thanks to our conscience, do we get a glimpse of our major and most obvious spiritual wounds.*

* *The Adam Complex.* Dee Margaret Pennock. Light and Life Publ. Co. Mpls, MN 2004.

Baptism is a training in dying to the old nature through daily repentance as we deny self and take up the cross to follow Jesus.

MEETING GOD IS MEETING TRUTH

Thus, self-knowledge is the ultimate victory. And self-knowledge itself begets the gentle virtue of humility which feasts on truth and does away with all the frantic efforts to cover up shortcomings to be what we are not.

Meeting God is meeting Truth. Meeting God in Truth disintegrates illusion. It exposes escapism as cowardice and fills us with God's joy, peace and truth.

We can create a false front and a glittering image, or we can be honest before God, before ourselves and others, about our weaknesses and allow God to transform us. But we will not have the energy to do both. We must choose one or the other.

Thus, the greatest of all sciences is KNOW THYSELF. It is a life-long task achievable only by the Father in the Son through the Holy Spirit.

> *Grant to us, O Lord, the knowledge of ourselves without which we can neither rightly repent nor seek to amend our lives. Help us to find our true identity in the Trinity as we come to confess humbly that each one of us is loved by God the Father, redeemed by God the Son and indwelt by God the Holy Spirit. We thank You for this–our true, God-given identity. Amen.*

POSTSCRIPT

So, do not think highly of yourself because of what you know about any art or science, but rather respect the knowledge that has been entrusted to you. If it seems to you that you know many things and that you are an expert in them, recognize nevertheless that there are many things that you do not know. Do not be high-minded, but admit your great ignorance. Why do you wish to think yourself better than others when you discover many people more learned and more practiced in God's ways than your are? If you want to learn something that will really help you, learn to see yourself as God sees you and not as you see yourself in the distorted mirror of your own self-importance. This is the greatest and most useful lesson we can learn: to know ourselves for what we truly are, to admit freely our weaknesses and failings, and to hold a humble opinion of ourselves because of them. Not to dwell on ourselves and always to think well and highly of others is great wisdom and perfection.

If you should see another person sin openly or commit some grave wrong, still you should not think yourself a better person by comparison, for you do not know how long you may remain in a good state. We are all frail, but think no one more frail than yourself.*

---

* *The Imitation of Christ: A Spiritual Commentary and Reader's Guide.* Dennis J. Billy. Christian Classics, Ave Maria Press. Notre Dame, IN. 2005.

FREE CATALOG

This is just one of the many books published by

Light and Life Publishing Company.

Request a **FREE** catalog to view our complete selection of items or visit us at **www.light-n-life.com**

☐ **YES!** *Please send me a free catalog.*

Name: _____

Address: _____

City, State, Zip: _____

Telephone: _____

Send to Light and Life Publishing Company:

by Mail   PO Box 26421 Minneapolis, MN 55426-0421
by Fax   888.925.3918
by Email   info@light-n-life.com